Matter, 1
Consciousness

Matter, Life and Consciousness

God and Science
in the Twenty-First Century

Three Essays and a Postscript

Carl Emery

HOPE BOOKS

Published by Hope Books

A CIP catalogue record for this book is available from the British Library.

ISBN 978-1-9996999-1-8

Book layout and cover design by Clare Brayshaw

Illustration 117594136 / Big Bang © Pollyw | Dreamstime.com

Prepared and printed by:

York Publishing Services Ltd
64 Hallfield Road
Layerthorpe
York YO31 7ZQ

Tel: 01904 431213

Website: www.yps-publishing.co.uk

To my wife, Lizzie

and

in loving memory of my father,
Jack Emery, 1913 – 2013

Contents

Preface

It is widely held today that to believe in God is not rational because rational belief is ruled out by what the natural sciences teach us. This view, 'scientism', is defined by the Oxford Dictionary as 'the belief that only knowledge obtained from scientific research is valid, and that notions or beliefs deriving from other sources, such as religion, should be discounted'. The three essays and Postscript which follow take a contrary view. They argue, first, that the reasons given by the atheist proponents of scientism for rejecting theistic belief as irrational are not compelling; and, secondly, that it can rationally be held that scientific knowledge actually supports theistic belief.

* * *

In Judeo-Christian theism, love is at the heart both of goodness and of 'God-ness'. Certainly, love – or compassion – is also at the heart of other theistic and non-theistic belief systems. But perhaps only in Christianity is love personified: God is seen not only as the benevolent and beneficent (and, hence, 'loving') creator of the universe but also as *love itself*. The foundational Christian statement that 'God is love' is reflected in the dual injunction to love God, and to love one's neighbour 'as oneself'. Again, the latter injunction – enshrining the so-called 'Golden Rule' requiring us to treat others as we would have them treat us – may be foundational to other belief systems, but it is particularly associated in the popular mind with theism in general and Christianity in particular.

Now, this association may or may not, in the twenty-first century, be conducive to the flourishing of the Golden Rule. For there is, in scientism, a more insidious tendency than merely to predispose people to think that belief in God is irrational, and therefore foolish. It is the tendency to link rejection of belief in God with rejection of the Golden Rule. Judeo-Christian theism proclaims that 'love is the ultimate and highest goal to which man can aspire…. The salvation of man is through love and in love'[1]. One can, of course, accept this while rejecting belief in God. But acceptance or rejection of both do tend to go together. While the essential point I am making in this book is that science does not defeat belief in God, my aim in making the point is not only to show that what is called a *sensus divinitatis* – a deep-seated conviction that there is a God – can be rationally defended; but also, in so doing, to remove any impediment which scientism may constitute to the whole-hearted pursuit of human salvation 'through love and in love'.

* * *

The three essays were published in the *Heythrop Journal* between 2013 and 2022 and are reprinted here with some corrections and additions. The essays focus on the philosophy underpinning, respectively, three areas of science: cosmology (under the heading 'Matter'), evolution ('Life'), and neuroscience ('Consciousness'). The thrust of the essays is that it is rational both to accept everything that the science in question tells us and at the same time to believe in God as the creator and sustainer of the natural world of which matter, life and consciousness are fundamental elements. Finally, in a brief Postscript, I consider the relation between science and the 'undeserved suffering argument' for atheism.

---

1   Viktor Frankl, *Man's Search for Meaning*, p 49.

1. Matter

Consciousness or the Physical Universe – Which Came First?

Historically, many have seen the intelligibility of the physical universe as showing that it is somehow ultimately dependent upon a conscious, intelligent, pre-existing being – 'God'. Today, however, many believe that modern advances in our scientific understanding of the origins and nature of the universe, and of the conscious, intelligent beings it contains, render God, as Laplace said, an 'unnecessary hypothesis'. This essay considers whether the findings of modern science do indeed diminish the plausibility of belief in a creator God. Or, on the contrary, whether there are features of current scientific understanding which may reasonably be thought to support the belief that conscious, intelligent being pre-existed the physical universe and caused it to be. In short: can science reasonably be thought to support the view that consciousness created the physical universe rather than that the physical universe created consciousness?

I. HOW THE QUESTION ARISES TODAY

The physical origin of the universe

As is well known, scientific theory supported by empirical observation currently paints the following broad cosmological picture.

Our observable universe, space and time, came into being from nothing material via a 'Big Bang' some 13.7 billion years ago. Immediately after the Big Bang the entire primordial content of the universe was intensely dense and hot. But almost immediately (in a process known as 'inflation') it expanded for a split second at an immense speed, cooling and becoming less dense. It has continued to expand, more slowly, ever since and is thought now to be destined in the distant future to accelerate exponentially to ultimate destruction. The Big Bang generated and energised the particles of matter which very soon formed the hydrogen and helium nuclei[1] which, in time,[2] became atoms – basic constituents of stars clustered into galaxies. There are perhaps hundreds of billions of galaxies, each galaxy itself containing hundreds of billions of stars and measuring hundreds of thousands of light years across.

Matter and the forces which act upon it (gravity, electro-magnetism and the strong and weak nuclear forces, together with the recently-discovered and little-understood expansion force of 'dark energy') behave uniformly in space and in time throughout the observable universe. This uniformity is described in terms of there being 'laws of nature' which govern not only everything which has occurred since the Big Bang but were themselves somehow responsible for generating the Big Bang.

How life emerged in a previously wholly inorganic universe remains a mystery. But what is now clear is that the inorganic environment had features which made it peculiarly suitable for life to emerge. An issue which continues to polarise opinion is whether one can usefully ask the question why the inorganic universe is, in Paul Davies'

---

1   Only hydrogen and helium nuclei (and trace amounts of deuterium and lithium) emerged from the period of nuclear fusion in the first few minutes after the Big Bang: see *The story of the element carbon* in section II, below.

2   Around 400,000 years after the Big Bang the universe had cooled sufficiently for protons to capture electrons, so allowing the formation of atoms.

words[3], 'just right for life'. Is the emergence of life and the evolution of conscious beings of any special significance or is it to be seen as simply another outcome of the operation of the physical laws just referred to? In particular, is there any special significance in the fact that there are intelligent beings in the universe who can understand ever more about how the universe came to be as it is, and about how they came to be part of it? Also, does life – including intelligent life – exist elsewhere than on Earth? Current indications are that it does – and in great abundance. For even in our own Milky Way galaxy of at least 100 billion sun-like stars, there are, according to recent estimates, some 20 billion Earth-size planets many of which may be suitable for life. And there are at least 100 billion galaxies in our observable universe governed by uniform physical laws. The chances seem small that in these circumstances intelligent life has evolved only on our tiny globe.

Cosmologists do, of course, acknowledge that questions arise as to how the universe came into being 'from nothing'. Since time, like space, began to exist only immediately after the Big Bang, it makes no sense to ask 'what happened before the Big Bang?' For there was no time for anything to happen in. Yet it does make sense to ask what caused the Big Bang and the physical laws and forces which generated it. Broadly, there are two possible types of answer. Either there was a natural propensity for the event to occur, or the cause of the event was extra- (or super-) natural. If it was a natural propensity, there is no logical necessity to do more than describe it. There is no logical basis for insisting that there must be a cause of the natural propensity any more than that there must be a cause of an extra- (or super-)

---

3   *The Goldilocks Enigma – Why is the Universe Just Right for Life?* (London: Penguin Books, 2007; hereafter, *GE*).

natural cause. So, for example, some scientists describe the natural propensity which they believe caused the Big Bang as a 'singularity'. This is essentially the conclusion of a mathematical projection back from what is known about the operation of laws and forces in the very early universe to a point of 'infinite curve and density'[4] beyond which further projection is impossible. Logically, the singularity may simply have existed: it may simply be the uncaused cause of the Big Bang and all that followed. But, equally, it may be the creation of pre-existing, conscious being.

Why might conscious being be thought to have created the physical universe?

Suppose that the laws and the forces which caused the Big Bang simply exist as 'brute facts'. Suppose too, for the moment, that the observable universe is all that there is.[5] On this basis, we are invited by materialists[6] to believe that the laws and the forces which govern the universe 'just happened' to be as they are and 'just happened' to cause life to emerge from inorganic matter. Of course, Richard Dawkins[7] and others have explained that the *evolution* of life from its primitive beginnings cannot be said likewise to have 'just happened'. For the driving force of organic evolution is natural selection – the natural propensity of those organisms which are best adapted to survive and reproduce in the environment in which they find themselves to survive best and to reproduce best in that environment. This is said

---

4   *GE* p 79.

5   Many scientists believe, on the contrary, that the observable universe is only an infinitesimal part of a 'multiverse' (see section IV below).

6   On 'materialism', see further, Essay 3 Part I.

7   *The Blind Watchmaker* (London: Longman, 1986).

to be the answer to Paley's[8] 'watchmaker' argument – the argument that a complex and well-designed organism such as *homo sapiens*, like a complex and well-designed machine, implies an intelligent and purposive designer.

But there is no process of natural selection in the inorganic world. Natural selection may be able to explain why birds have wings and many creatures have eyes. But it has no application to the question of why the laws and forces which govern, and have governed, inorganic matter are as they are – producing the complex, intelligible universe which we observe and, in particular, the organic life from which intelligent beings have evolved. And many continue to believe that this complexity and intelligibility are the product of pre-existing, conscious, intelligent being rather than of a cosmic lottery governed by pure chance. The question is, then, whether current scientific understanding of the physical universe may reasonably be thought to support such belief or, on the contrary, does it suggest that things are as they are simply because they happen to be so, or for some other reason?

II. 'FINE TUNING' IN THE UNIVERSE

Laws, Values and Interactions

Scientific laws are general statements of relationships between physical phenomena. Newton's law of gravity, for example, states that the force of gravitational attraction exerted by one object upon another is directly proportional to the product of their masses, and inversely proportional to the square of the distance between them (so, if the distance between the objects doubles, the force diminishes four-fold). The electromagnetic attraction or repulsion between two objects varies in like fashion. Clearly, such laws by

---

8   William Paley, *Natural Theology* (1802).

themselves tell us nothing about the actual strength of the force in question in any specific case. To discover this, we have to insert values (or quantities) into the equations. These values can be obtained only by empirical observation – by measurement.

As will appear below, the actual strengths of forces such as gravity and electromagnetism are among a relatively small number of values critical to the configuration of the physical universe. If they were significantly different from what they are, the universe would demonstrably be a very different place from what it is. In particular, many of the features which allow life to emerge and to evolve would be absent. And it is not the values of particular forces alone which account for things being as they are. It is also the relationships – the numerical ratios – between the strengths of different forces. For example, as we shall see, it can be shown that there are features of the universe critical to the existence of life which depend precisely upon the ratio between the strengths of the gravitational and electromagnetic forces being as it is.

For present purposes the central point is this: it is not understood why the values which are observed and which, taken together, produce an environment suitable for the emergence and evolution of life forms, are what they are. They are not, so to say, dictated by theory. So far as is currently understood, they just happen to be as they are. These so-called 'free parameters' could, theoretically, be different; and if they were, life as it is could not exist. But they are not, and it does.

This is what is meant when it is said that the universe is 'fine-tuned' (or 'just right') for life to emerge. But two crucial points must be made at once: first, the statement just made that the free parameters could, theoretically, be different is true as far as current theory goes. It is obviously also true that in the future some new unifying theory may emerge which shows that the parameters are not in this sense 'free' but, on the contrary, could not be otherwise. This issue will be pursued in section IV, below. The second point is that to speak of 'fine tuning' does not necessarily imply that there is a conscious fine-tuner. This essay is concerned precisely with the question whether or not there is a basis for believing that there is such a conscious fine-tuner or universe designer. At present our concern is simply to give some examples of the phenomenon of fine tuning of numbers and ratios.

Examples of fine tuning – why there can be stars and planets – the cosmic numbers 'Q', 'N' and 'λ'

Planets such as Earth, with an environment suitable for the emergence and evolution of life, orbit sun-like stars in 'solar systems'. One finely-tuned number and two force ratios of the kind mentioned above are critical to the existence of stars and planets.

(1) The number 'Q', and the ratio, 'N', between the strengths of gravity and electromagnetism

The primordial matter in the early universe consisted of 'a plasma of freely-moving atomic components – protons, neutrons and electrons'[9]. The density of these microscopic quantum particles[10] fluctuates continuously. The extent of these quantum density fluctuations is very small (about 1 in 100,000 or 10^{-5} and denoted by the letter 'Q'[11]). It is thought that during the split second of extremely rapid 'inflation'

---

9   *GE* p 57.
10   The nature of quantum particles is explored below in section III, THE 'QUANTUM TO CLASSICAL' PHENOMENON.
11   *GE* p 165.

immediately after the Big Bang these small fluctuations were manifested as more and less dense areas of the embryo universe. Under the stronger gravitational force exerted by the denser areas the record of these fluctuations became writ ever larger in the expanding universe, those denser areas appearing as the 'ripples' (galaxy seeds) observable on the famous 2003 WMAP picture of the universe as it was at about 380,000 years after the Big Bang. As Martin Rees observes in *Just Six Numbers*[12]:

> The fabric of our universe depends on [the] number Q. If Q were ... smaller, the universe would be inert and structureless; if Q were much larger, it would be a violent place, in which no stars or solar systems could survive, dominated by vast black holes.

The number Q is, then, itself finely-tuned in the sense that Q is as it needs to be for the development of an environment (galaxies containing solar systems) in which life is possible. But the efficacy of Q in turn depends upon a further piece of fine tuning – the ratio between the strengths of the forces of gravity and electromagnetism. For it is this ratio which determines the environment within which Q has the effects above described. If the ratio – and so the environment – were different, Q would not have the effects which it does. How is this the case?

Electromagnetism operates within atoms to maintain their structure – the positively charged nucleus orbited by negatively charged electrons. Electromagnetism is hugely stronger than gravity: about 10^{36} times – a ratio denoted by the letter 'N'. This disparity is counter-intuitive: we experience gravity as strongly as we do because its force is cumulative: the more matter there is, the stronger is

---

12 (London: Phoenix) at p 3. For detail, see ch 8.

its gravity; whereas the net force of electromagnetism is much reduced by the interaction of positive and negative charges, 'so gravity "gains" relative to electrical forces in larger objects'[13]. The attractive effect of gravity at atomic level is thus completely overwhelmed by the effect of electromagnetism. But at larger scales, gravity is felt ever more powerfully.

It is N, the 10^{36} ratio – expressing the weakness of gravity relative to electromagnetism – which is critical in determining the effect of Q – the measure of the continuous fluctuations of the density of the elementary, quantum, constituents of matter. Were gravity stronger relative to electromagnetism, the galaxy-seeding effect of Q (described above) would have been fatally compromised.[14] And it is N which determines the relative effects of the two forces at all levels – and which, thus, determines many critical features of the observable universe, including the size, thermal properties and life-span of stars and their planets – and thus the time available for organic evolution.[15]

In short, then: the number Q is as it needs to be to produce a universe in which life is possible. But Q has the effect it does because the ratio N is as it is, governing the interaction of gravity and electromagnetism at the atomic level at which Q operates. If Q is the seed, N is the soil in which it flourishes.

---

13 Rees, *Just Six Numbers*, p 31; see also, *GE* p 163.
14 Max Tegmark and Martin Rees, 'Why Is the Cosmic Microwave Background Fluctuation Level 10^{-5}?', *Astrophysical Journal*, June 1998.
15 Rees, *ibid*, ch 3. See also, *GE* pp 163-164.

(2) The relationship between the strengths of gravity and dark energy ('λ')

Also critical to the existence of a universe containing planets hospitable to life is the relationship of gravity to another force whose strength has only recently been ascertained.

Einstein at first believed that the universe was held at a constant size by an expansionary (anti-gravitational) force whose strength was just right to prevent gravity from causing the universe to collapse under its own weight. He later acknowledged that Hubble's observations in the 1920s indicated that the universe was not static, but expanding – albeit at an ever-decreasing rate. But in 1998, using data from the Hubble Space Telescope, it was discovered from observation of very distant supernovas (explosions as massive stars collapse)[16] that the rate at which the universe is expanding is in fact increasing rather than decreasing. The expansionary force responsible for this increasing rate of expansion is referred to as 'dark energy' and may be thought of as a kind of negative pressure, or tension, in inter-galactic space. Its nature (like that of 'dark matter' which, apparently, far exceeds 'ordinary' matter in both mass and, therefore, gravitational effect[17]) is not yet understood. But measurements have shown that, relative to the strength of gravity, the strength of dark energy (a value denoted by the Greek letter 'λ') is very low, thus enabling the formation of galaxies and their continuing existence for a period long enough for life to emerge and evolve as it has. But Davies observes[18] that:

---

16 See further below.
17 Rees, *Just Six Numbers*, ch 6. (It is calculated that dark energy and dark matter together make up around 96% of the mass of the observable universe. The remaining 4% is the mass of 'ordinary' matter: *GE* p 139.)
18 *GE* p 170.

> [I]f the magnitude of the dark energy were only moderately larger than the observed value, it would have frustrated the formation of galaxies.... So our existence depends on dark energy not being too large.

More fine tuning – the story of the element carbon

Because it occurs in all living tissue and readily combines with other elements critical for life-formation, carbon is often said to be the key life-giving element. Both its emergence and its dissemination are processes which display a high degree of fine tuning.

(1) Nuclear fusion in the early universe: the strength of the weak nuclear force and the ratio of hydrogen to helium

As will be explained below, carbon is made in stars by the fusion of helium nuclei. The fuel for this nuclear fusion process is hydrogen. The amount of carbon in the universe thus depends upon the proportion of hydrogen, the fuel for its manufacture, to helium, its raw material. This proportion, established during the period of nuclear fusion of hydrogen into helium in the first few minutes after the Big Bang, is 75:25 in favour of hydrogen – a proportion which gives just enough helium for the manufacture of the amount of carbon which has been sufficient for the emergence of life, and just enough hydrogen both for the nuclear fusion in stars which has produced that amount of carbon and for the making, with oxygen, of life-grounding water.

It is now understood[19] that this critical hydrogen-to-helium ratio itself depends upon the finely-tuned strength of the weak nuclear force which operates within atomic nuclei to transmute neutrons into protons. In the

---

19   *GE* pp 161-162.

few minutes of nuclear fusion shortly after the Big Bang the weak nuclear force transmuted unstable primordial neutrons into protons (hydrogen nuclei). But some of these neutrons escaped transmutation by combining with protons to form stable helium nuclei. Had the weak nuclear force been stronger than it is (transmuting neutrons more quickly), less helium and more hydrogen would have resulted; vice versa had it been weaker. Either way, 'the chemical make-up of the universe would be very different, and with much poorer prospects for life'[20].

(2) Nuclear fusion in stars: the strength of the strong nuclear force and the making of carbon

Only hydrogen and helium nuclei (and trace amounts of deuterium and lithium) emerged from the period of nuclear fusion in the first few minutes after the Big Bang. Carbon and almost all of the other elements found in nature are created by nuclear fusion in star cores. In this process protons collide at high speed and are forced and held together by the strong nuclear force which overcomes the protons' electrical repulsion. But carbon is unique among the elements in the following way. The strong nuclear force causes the single-proton nuclei of hydrogen to fuse readily to produce helium nuclei: 2-proton, 2-neutron 'alpha particles'. But when two of these helium nuclei collide at fusion temperatures what is produced is an unstable isotope of beryllium which, without more, would decay (under the protons' electrical repulsion) before a third helium nucleus could collide with it to produce a stable (6-proton, 6-neutron, 'triple alpha') carbon nucleus. In stellar nuclear fusion this decay is in fact delayed long enough for carbon to be formed by the addition of a third

---

20 *Ibid.*

helium nucleus. The delay is caused by a momentary surge of energy in the beryllium nucleus generated by so-called 'quantum resonance'. At fusion temperatures this is a continual process of rapid increase in the frequency of quantum density fluctuation[21] to a high point (or 'spike') followed by an immediate, equally rapid, decrease. The level of this resonance is determined by the strength of the strong nuclear force relative to the electromagnetic repulsion between colliding protons.

As Davies says[22]: 'If the strong force were slightly stronger or slightly weaker (by maybe as little as 1 per cent), then the binding energies of the nuclei would change', the 'triple alpha process' of carbon production could not occur and life could not exist in our universe. Fred Hoyle, who in the early 1950s calculated the level of the resonance, famously observed that this unlikely degree of precision in the interaction between the strong nuclear and electromagnetic forces during nuclear fusion made the appearance of carbon look like a 'put-up job'.

(3) Dissemination of carbon as stars collapse: strength of weak nuclear force again

As noted in (1) above, the strength of the weak nuclear force was critical in producing the 75:25 hydrogen/helium ratio upon which the amount of both carbon and hydrogen, and so the existence of life in the universe, ultimately depends. As will now be explained, it is critical also in facilitating the dissemination of carbon and its appearance on earth (and in other life-friendly environments).

When a star's supply of hydrogen becomes insufficient for nuclear fusion, the star collapses and may then explode

---

21   See above.
22   *GE* p 157.

producing a short-lived, intensely bright 'supernova'. In the collapse, material is violently compressed and the weak nuclear force causes protons to transmute into neutrons (cf above for neutron to proton transmutation), thereby releasing particles called neutrinos. These neutrinos are emitted from the supernova in high-pressure streams which create a pathway for the passage of carbon and other heavy elements into space. This functioning of the neutrino streams results directly from the finely-tuned strength of the weak nuclear force. If the weak force were weaker, the neutrinos would lack the strength to create the pathway; if stronger, they would react with other particles in the stellar core and would not be emitted into space. 'Either way, the dissemination of carbon and other heavy elements needed for life ... would be compromised.'[23]

* * *

It is evident that the existence of life as we know it depends upon features of the observable universe which themselves depend upon the strengths of and ratios between the five known forces: gravity, dark energy, electromagnetism and the strong and weak nuclear forces. The observed values of these strengths and ratios cannot, at present, be explained by reference to any theory. Yet, were any one or more of these values significantly different – less finely-tuned – the universe would not be intelligible as it is, nor would it contain intelligent observers to whom its intelligibility is apparent.

Section IV below will consider the relevance of fine tuning to the question whether the findings of modern science may reasonably be thought to support the belief that conscious intelligent being pre-existed and caused the

23   *GE* p 160.

universe to be. But first it is necessary to say something about a different kind of fine tuning.

III. THE 'QUANTUM TO CLASSICAL' PHENOMENON – TUNING TO THE PERCEPTIONS OF CONSCIOUS BEINGS

The point to be made here is essentially this. The fundamental – 'quantum' – constituents of matter do not behave in the clear and predictable manner in which, at everyday level, we perceive matter to behave. Yet they do behave in a manner which produces the clear and predictable behaviour which we conscious beings perceive. It will be suggested that this can be seen as a kind of fine tuning which is no less remarkable than that dealt with above.

* * *

At the level of our everyday perception, matter behaves as described by the laws of Newtonian (or 'classical') physics. Essentially, we see any given material object as being located in one particular place at one particular time: it is now here or it is there. And, generally, we can make firm and accurate predictions about where it will be in the immediate future: it behaves deterministically.

It is now well-established that this clear and reliable material world of our everyday perception is not the material world which we will see if we very greatly magnify the material object which we are looking at. The atoms of which all matter is composed are almost unimaginably small, but the fundamental 'quantum' particles of which atoms themselves are made 'are at least 100 million times smaller than the atoms'[24]. The nuclei of atoms consist of protons and (the single-proton hydrogen nucleus apart)

---

24 Polkinghorne, *Quantum Theory, a Very Short Introduction* (Oxford: Oxford University Press), p 39.

neutrons, both of which are themselves made up of a type of these fundamental particles called quarks. The atomic nucleus is orbited by a different type of fundamental particle, the electron. These fundamental constituents of matter do not behave clearly and deterministically according to Newtonian principles; instead, they behave in a manner which the Nobel prize-winning physicist Richard Feynman described as uncertain and probabilistic.[25]

The uncertainty is exemplified by the characteristic of quantum particles that they exist ordinarily in a state of 'superposition' – they are, at any given moment, neither exclusively here nor exclusively there: they are, although indivisible, to some extent both here and there. The notion of superposition is dramatically illustrated by the so-called 'double slits experiment'[26]. In this experiment, a stream of electrons[27] is fired towards a screen in which there are two well-separated slits through which the electrons can pass. Some distance beyond the slit screen is a detector screen which records the impact of those electrons which have passed through the slit screen. Since electrons are indivisible, one would expect that each electron which passes through the screen would pass through one slit or the other. And if a detector is placed very near each slit, then this is indeed what is observed. But if the electrons are left unobserved until they hit the more distant detector screen, the record of their impact shows that each indivisible electron passed through both slits. As John Polkinghorne has remarked[28], 'In terms of classical intuition this is a nonsense conclusion. In terms of quantum theory's superposition principle, however, it makes perfect sense.'

25 Feynman, *The Character of Physical Law*, ch 6.
26 Described with pellucid clarity by Feynman, *ibid.*
27 Photons may be used instead.
28 *Loc cit* p 24.

The superpositional character of matter at its fundamental level reflects the fact that at this level it behaves not only like a particle but also like a wave. It is a feature of this 'wave-particle duality' that if one measures[29] precisely the (particle-like) position of a quantum entity at a particular moment one cannot simultaneously precisely measure its (wave-like) momentum or any other variable property of the quantum particle, such as its spin. The more precisely its position (say) is identified, the less precisely can one simultaneously identify its other variable properties; and complete certainty as to one variable necessarily goes with maximum uncertainty as to others. This is Heisenberg's 'uncertainty principle' which yields the following further profound contrast between quantum and classical behaviour of matter. A particular feature of classical behaviour is the so-called 'arrow of time': at classical level the behaviour of matter is perceived within an irreversible time sequence. There is no such perception at quantum level: '[the] film would make equal sense if it were run forwards or backwards'[30].

The behaviour of matter at this fundamental microscopic ('micro') level is non-classical also in that it is probabilistic rather than deterministic. At a certain level of largeness (perhaps the size of larger molecules such as DNA and above) most groupings of quantum particles behave predictably, according to Newton's laws, when observed at everyday, macroscopic ('macro'), level. In contrast, at micro levels matter behaves unpredictably. This unpredictability is confined within certain limits: the range of probable behaviour of a given quantum entity (its 'probability

---

29 On this momentary measurement of a variable property of a quantum particle such as its position, see further below.

30 Polkinghorne, above, p 49; Rees, *Just Six Numbers*, p 152.

amplitudes') is expressed by the so-called Schrödinger equation. It is important to stress that the unpredictability of quantum behaviour is held to be what one may call 'true' or 'real' or 'objective'[31] unpredictability. In the world of classical physics, if an outcome is unpredictable (like the toss of a coin or throw of dice) it is so because we do not have enough information about all the relevant circumstances governing the outcome; but the behaviour of a quantum particle is unpredictable because its developing course is generally held[32] to be not governed by cause and effect, but to be (within the relevant probability amplitudes) truly a matter of 'pure chance'.

The 'quantum to classical' problem

If quantum behaviour is, as Feynman often insisted, mysterious, it is also something of a mystery that matter behaves classically when observed and experienced at everyday level. For consider:

- Matter is made up entirely of quantum entities ('wave-particles') which always and everywhere behave non-classically. For it is emphatically *not* the case that groupings of quantum particles above a certain size *cease* to behave in a quantum fashion and *instead* behave classically.

- In fact, if one 'zooms-in' sufficiently closely on *any* matter – a pool of water, a chunk of rock, a piece

---

31 As opposed to the 'subjective' unpredictability which reflects an individual subject's limited knowledge of circumstances.

32 David Bohm's theory of quantum determinism has not found wide support in the scientific community. But for the possibility of quantum *nondeterministic* (or probabilistic) causation, see G. E. M. Anscombe, 'Causality and Determination' (her inaugural professorial lecture), Cambridge University Press, 1971.

of flesh – what one will see is, exclusively, quantum behaviour. That this is so is attested by empirical evidence of the most compelling and unequivocal kind.

- For as Feynman has written: '[quantum] theory describes all the phenomena of the physical world [he instances 'gasoline burning in automobiles, foam and bubbles, the hardness of salt or copper, the stiffness of steel'] except the gravitational effect ... and radioactive phenomena'[33]. And the theory matches observation to an extraordinarily high degree. For example, experimental measurement of the magnetic force of an electron matches the predictions of quantum theory to an accuracy of a human hair's thickness in the distance from Los Angeles to New York.[34] By comparison, the predictions of Newtonian theory correspond with experimental observation only approximately.

- In other words, the behaviour of matter which we observe as clear and deterministic at macro level is far more accurately described by observation at micro level which shows it to be unclear and probabilistic.

- Nevertheless, at everyday level this continuing quantum behaviour is unnoticeable. As observed above, quantum entities are at least 100 million times smaller than atoms. Because of the scale of things, we do not observe quantum behaviour at everyday, macro, level. We observe, as it were, its opposite: uncertainty and probability at micro level

---

33 Feynman, *QED: The Strange Theory of Light and Matter* (London: Penguin Books, 1992), Introduction.

34 *Ibid.*

translate into clear and deterministic behaviour at everyday level.

How can this be the case?

It is not fully understood how the quantum behaviour of elementary particles can give rise to 'classical' behaviour in large systems – 'how it can be', as Polkinghorne says, 'that the quantum constituents of the physical world, such as quarks and ... electrons, whose behaviour is cloudy and fitful, can give rise to the macroscopic world of everyday experience, which seems so clear and reliable'[35].

It is, however, known[36] that background radiation in the environment contributes significantly to the emergence of classical behaviour through a process known as quantum decoherence which Polkinghorne defines as 'an environmental effect on quantum systems that is capable of rapidly inducing almost classical behaviour'[37]. This is part, but evidently not the whole, of the explanation. So a problem remains.

One possible route to a solution is as follows. Laboratory observation of a quantum particle can momentarily measure and record its precise position (or its momentum, or whatever other variable property of the quantum particle, e.g. its spin, is measured) as if it were a 'classical' particle – though immediately after the measurement is made the position (or other measured variable) changes and becomes once again uncertain. This measurement process thus records a momentary 'classicality' of position (or other measured variable) of the measured particle – a momentarily fixed, knowable state (an 'eigenstate'). The so-

---

35 Polkinghorne (above), p 43.

36 Ibid.

37 Polkinghorne, p 96. Research into this phenomenon has been active since the 1980s.

called 'Copenhagen interpretation' of quantum mechanics postulates that this momentary appearance of classicality is somehow induced by the largeness and complexity of the measuring apparatus. Extrapolating from this, it seems possible that it is the size and complexity of large and complex systems themselves which somehow accounts for their sustained classical behaviour as observed at everyday macro level.

Thus, while quantum particles do not behave classically, they routinely and predictably group themselves into large systems which, when observed at everyday level, do behave classically. There is a body of theory which predicts *that* this routine grouping with its attendant classical behaviour will occur as we perceive it to do. But *how* this classical, deterministic, behaviour of large quantum systems arises is not fully understood. Nevertheless, in so far as it does routinely arise in accordance with theory, its occurrence may be seen as a case of cause (large groupings of quantum entities) and effect (classical behaviour of those groupings when observed at everyday level). In this sense one may say that *the deterministic behaviour of matter at everyday level is predetermined to emerge from the non-deterministic behaviour of its quantum constituents.*

It is suggested that the fact that at everyday level matter behaves clearly and predictably whereas fundamentally its behaviour is uncertain and probabilistic can be seen as a kind of fine tuning. What we may label 'quantum-to-classical' fine tuning is a different kind from that dealt with above – the action and interaction of particles and forces which has, improbably, led to the appearance of life and the evolution of conscious intelligent beings. The emergence of classical from quantum behaviour of matter is 'fine tuning' in the sense that it allows the conscious intelligent beings who have evolved to perceive, and in some measure to understand, the observable universe. In short, it allows the physical world to be perceived as intelligible by intelligent beings.

IV. FINE TUNING AS EVIDENCE OF CONSCIOUS CREATION

How does our universe come to be finely-tuned?

This question requires a sharp focus. As the starting point of this 'how?' enquiry, take the notion, mentioned above, of a 'singularity' – a physical propensity for a 'Big Bang' to occur. For the moment, do not ask 'how does that propensity come to be?' Ask instead how life emerges from the Big Bang and its aftermath. Leave aside the awkward fact that scientists have not yet been able to explain how life emerges from inorganic matter. Assume for the purposes of the discussion what is highly probable – that scientists will sooner or later discover this. So, take it that we have a physical propensity for a Big Bang to occur; and assume that we can describe more or less the physical processes which lead from Big Bang to the emergence of life; and that the theory of evolution by random[38] mutation and natural selection explains how primitive life develops over time into highly complex life forms including conscious intelligent beings. In this context, what is the 'how?' question asking? Can we not simply say that the above analysis explains how our universe comes to be as it is and to contain conscious intelligent beings who can understand these things?

A difficulty which many find with this answer is its apparent treatment of the fine tuning described in the previous two sections as simply an assemblage of fortuitous cosmic facts which, neither singly nor collectively, call

---

38 See *Randomness and Chance* in Essay 2, below, p. 38.

for any special explanation. But chance does not seem to operate in this way[39]. If one week someone wins the National Lottery jackpot on the purchase of a single ticket, one will no doubt attribute the success to chance. If that person enjoys the same success each week for many weeks, one will certainly attribute that to the intervention of some conscious agent. Experience tells us that chance does not produce such a sequence. On a similar basis, it may fairly be said that the burden of offering some explanation, other than chance, of fine tuning in the universe lies upon those who decline to attribute it ultimately to the intervention of some conscious agent – to the deliberate action of pre-existing, conscious, intelligent being. Such, certainly, was the view of the authorities in the Soviet Union who discouraged work on the question of why the universe is fine-tuned for the emergence of life – for, as Davies says, 'It was an embarrassment – it looked too much like the work of a Cosmic Designer'[40].

If, then, the choice for explaining fine tuning is between chance and conscious, intelligent, pre-existing being – 'God' – many feel (some reluctantly) that God wins. But an alternative approach is to postulate that fine tuning can be wholly and satisfactorily explained by purely physical processes. Two very different varieties of such approach will now be considered.

(1) Fine tuning as a feature of an 'ultimate theory of everything'

One way of explaining away the appearance of conscious fine tuning is to argue that this appearance merely reflects the fact that current theoretical understanding of the observable universe is, so to say, 'piece-meal'. For, it is said,

---

39 But cf (2) below, on 'multiverse' theory.

40 *GE* p 172.

scientists may sooner or later discover an adequate 'theory of everything': a theory which will show how all current observationally-supported theories are simply constituents of a single over-arching theory which will explain why all observed values and ratios are necessarily as they are.

Such a theory would show us that things – including what we currently see as finely-tuned particular values and ratios – could not, scientifically speaking, be otherwise than they are. In the context of this hypothetical comprehensive theory, the value of the quantum resonance spike which explains how carbon came to be made would no longer seem to be a 'put-up job'; and the critical ratios of the forces of gravity and electromagnetism, or of gravity and dark energy, would no longer appear inexplicably, suspiciously, like the temperature of Baby Bear's porridge, 'just right' for life. All would follow from this over-arching theory of everything.

But, of course, the question would remain of how the universe came to be governed by such a theory. The theory would show that the physical characteristics of the universe which we now see as 'fine tuning' could not indeed be other than they are. But one would still be entitled to ask 'why *this* universe, explicable by *this* theory? Why not another universe and another theory? Or why not no universe at all?' In terms of answering the 'fine tuning' question, the discovery of a 'theory of everything' of this sort simply brings us back to a choice between regarding it either as a brute fact – a fortuitous 'given' – or as the work of God.

But there is another quite different type of 'ultimate theory' which must now be considered.

(2) Fine tuning as simply 'observer selection effect' in a multiverse

Many cosmologists[41] today think that what appears to be fine tuning is actually an illusion induced by a sort of cosmological myopia. They conjecture that our observable universe is in fact only one, so-called 'pocket', universe in a cosmos which contains countless billions of such pocket universes. The cosmos is thus a 'multiverse'. Only some, perhaps a very few, pocket universes will turn out by chance to have the physical characteristics required for sustaining life and evolving intelligent observers. Since, *ex hypothesi*, those few pocket universes will be 'just right' for sustaining life and evolving intelligent observers, the fact that they are and have done so requires no special explanation. What seems from our extremely limited perspective to be extraordinarily fine tuning is, in the vastly wider perspective of the multiverse, no more than the inexorable operation of chance – just as a very few players will beat the huge odds against winning the lottery jackpot.

The basis of multiverse theory (there are a number of different versions) is the application of Heisenberg's quantum uncertainty principle[42] to current thinking about the very early universe, in particular the split second of 'inflation' immediately following the Big Bang. Briefly, the primordial quantum flux is regarded as inherently inflationary. Inflation manifests a, perhaps eternally, recurring cycle of uncertainty of the variables in the behaviour of quantum entities. Each pocket universe is the product of one single episode[43] of 'Big Bang' inflation among billions; it has been calculated (by reference to the possible range of outcomes contained within quantum

---

41   Davies says 'a growing minority' (*GE*, p 298).
42   For this, and quantum theory generally, see III above.
43   Rees, *Just Six Numbers*, p 147.

probability amplitudes) that the number of such pocket universes is likely vastly to exceed the number of atoms in our own pocket universe.[44] And each pocket universe develops differently from the others. As in each episode of inflation the quantum vacuum expands and cools, its primordial 'symmetries' are broken in different ways and with different outcomes ('domain structures') in and between the forces operating within each pocket universe.[45] Given the unimaginably large number of possible pocket universes, it is entirely unsurprising that ours will exist, with its apparently fine-tuned, but actually random, parameters which make it 'just right for life'.

Since, on this approach, our observable universe is the only pocket universe which we can observe, it is immediately evident that the notion of empirical verification of multiverse theory presents formidable difficulties. Certainly, at present, the epistemological status of the theory is nearer to theology than to science.

Conclusion: cosmology and religion today

Rees summarises the position as follows:

> If the underlying laws determine all the key numbers uniquely, so that no other universe is mathematically consistent with those laws, then we would have to accept that the 'tuning' was [either] a brute fact, or providence. On the other hand, the ultimate theory might permit a multiverse whose evolution is punctuated by repeated Big Bangs; the underlying physical laws, applying throughout the multiverse, may then permit diversity in the individual universes.[46]

---

44 One estimate suggests 10^{500} pocket universes compared with the mere 10^{80} atoms in our observable universe (*GE*, p 192).

45 *Ibid*, pp 184-185 *passim*.

46 Rees, *loc cit*, p 174.

Briefly, then: unless fine tuning is simply how things chance to be ('brute fact'), it reflects either the working of 'providence' or the fact that our vast observable universe is just one of billions of pocket universes comprising a multiverse. More briefly still: it seems that to explain fine tuning we must back either chance, or God, or a multiverse.[47]

This essay asks whether there are features of current scientific understanding of the origin and character of the physical universe – in particular of its suitability for the emergence of life, and for the evolution of intelligent beings – which may reasonably be thought to support the belief that the universe is the product of consciousness rather than the reverse. That this belief today offers one of the three widely-held alternative rational[48] explanations of fine tuning is surely enough to warrant an affirmative answer to the question. In itself, clearly, the belief that the universe is the product of consciousness raises, but does not begin to answer, numerous and varied questions regarding the origin and nature of this 'consciousness'. But clearly too, one line of answers to these questions leads to monotheism. So, for Christians and others, this view of fine tuning can offer a way of reconciling the findings of modern science with the foundations, at any rate, of their religious belief. For if science and religion are equally concerned in the search for truth they must be reconciled.

---

47   In *GE*, ch 10, Davies explores a possible third scientific approach (alternative to chance and multiverse) based essentially on the lack of an 'arrow of time' in quantum theory. This may allow 'later' (in 'classical' terms) events to influence 'earlier' ones. In this way, he suggests, the universe may come to be understood as a closed system or 'causal loop' which requires no explanation of its existence or intelligibility other than that it exists and is intelligible. See further, Essay 3 Part II, section on *Quantum mechanics and natural teleology*.

48   Davies, *GE*, p 225.

To be sure, things may look different in the future, as scientific understanding develops. If multiverse thinking becomes scientific orthodoxy, our perspective upon what we now call fine tuning will change, along with both scientific and religious understandings. But for now:

> It may be frustrating to acknowledge, but we are simply at the point in the history of human thought at which we find ourselves, and our successors will make discoveries and develop forms of understanding of which we have not dreamt. Humans are addicted to the hope for a final reckoning, but intellectual humility requires that we resist the temptation to assume that tools of the kind we now have are in principle sufficient to understand the universe as a whole.[49]

---

49 Thomas Nagel, *Mind and Cosmos: Why the Materialist Neo-Darwinian Conception of Nature is Almost Certainly False* (Oxford: Oxford University Press, 2012), p 3. Like Davies, Nagel argues that we should seek a natural, not an extra- (or super-) natural, explanation of the intelligibility of the universe. But, unlike Davies, Nagel suggests (p 32, *passim*) that the natural explanation will turn out to be not wholly materialistic but will take account of the fundamentally 'physical and ... mental character of the universe' (p 69). Nagel's approach is examined in Essay 3.

2. Life

God and the Design of Organisms

Does the design of organisms indicate the existence of a conscious designer – God?

Reviewing Jerry Coyne's *Why Evolution is True*,[1] Richard Dawkins 'def[ied] any reasonable person to read this marvellous book and still take seriously the "breathtaking inanity" that is intelligent design "theory".'[2] Coyne summarises 'the modern theory[3] of evolution' thus:

> Life on Earth evolved gradually beginning with one primitive species – perhaps a self-replicating molecule – that lived more than 3.5 billion years ago; it then branched out over time, throwing off many new and diverse species and the mechanism for most (but not all[4]) evolutionary change is natural selection.[5]

The phrase 'breathtaking inanity' was used by an American judge to describe the policy of a Schools Board which required its teachers to offer intelligent design (ID) 'theory' as a scientific alternative to the theory of evolution. The ID 'alternative' is that species did not evolve: the complexity and variety of species can be explained only on the basis that they were individually designed and created by God.

---

1 Oxford University Press, 2009; hereafter, 'Coyne'.
2 Dawkins' view appears on the cover of the hardback edition of Coyne.
3 Darwin's theory of evolution by variation and natural selection has been much elaborated by post-Darwinian scientific advances, particularly the development of the science of genetics (see below).
4 'Genetic drift' is an additional mechanism with probably only a minor effect on evolution (Coyne, p 14).
5 Coyne, p 3.

This ID theory, in contradicting compelling contrary evidence, is correctly seen as demeaning both science and religion and as putting them at loggerheads. The difficulty is that some scientists, among whom Dawkins is prominent, take the view that evolutionary theory not only rules out alternative scientific accounts of the origin of species but also rules out belief in a God of whose existence the design of organisms, amongst other things, may be taken to be an indication. Dawkins says that to believe in God is not rational: he speaks of 'The God Delusion'[6].

It will be argued in this essay that to believe in God, and to believe that the existence of God is indicated by the design of organisms, are beliefs which may rationally be held. This is not to deny that it may be rational to believe that there is no God: it may be true that there are not compelling reasons to believe in God. But it is certainly false that there are compelling reasons not to.

* * *

Propositions about God are not scientifically verifiable or falsifiable, for they are not scientific hypotheses. The question is whether there are, nevertheless, valid (that is, sound or defensible, well-grounded) reasons to support the propositions that God exists and that the existence of God is indicated by the design of organisms. A widely held view is that there are not. This view is sometimes based on the argument that in the light of scientific knowledge, these propositions are overwhelmingly improbable: this argument will be examined below in section I, EVOLUTION AND DESIGN. The view may also reflect the conviction that only beliefs based on empirical observation are rational, that beliefs which are not empirically verifiable or falsifiable

---

6   The title of his book of 2006.

are not rational – they are 'acts of faith'. A third basis for the view that there are no valid reasons to hold that God exists is that, while in principle there may be valid reasons which are not empirically based, in fact none of the reasons advanced to support the proposition that God exists are valid. These arguments will be examined in section II, RATIONAL BELIEF.

I. EVOLUTION AND DESIGN

Richard Dawkins thinks that evolution provides compelling evidence of a universe without divine design.[7] Why does he think this?

The argument against the view that the existence of God is indicated by the design of organisms runs essentially as follows. It can be shown by a number of different types of evidence (particularly geological, palaeontological, genetic, embryological) that the design – the scheme or arrangement which governs the functioning – of any existing organism is derived from the design of previously existing organisms but that the process of 'derivation' is too-much governed by random and contingent events to be reasonably capable of being regarded as pre-planned. In particular, there is abundant evidence that the ability (or 'fitness') of some individuals to survive and to reproduce better than others in the environment in which they find themselves reflects slightly different genetic characteristics; that these genetic differences are acquired by those individuals randomly[8] in the course of post-conception cell multiplication and are transmissible reproductively to their own offspring;

---

7   The sub-title of Dawkins' book *The Blind Watchmaker* (Longman, 1986) is *Why the evidence of evolution reveals a universe without design.*

8   See *Randomness and Chance*, below.

and that these 'fitter' individuals and their offspring will naturally form an ever-larger proportion of the population. Thus, the design of organisms cannot be seen as the product of a preconceived plan: as the work of a conscious designer, 'God'. The design of organisms is, instead, the product of an unconscious natural process: the work of 'evolution'.

The science of genetics is at the core of current understanding of the process of organic evolution. The following summary may be a helpful preliminary to assessing the view that evolution rules out divine design.

DNA, genes and chromosomes

Beneath the variety and complexity of organic life there is a degree of uniformity and simplicity. Every cell of every organism contains molecules of DNA which is composed of just five elements: carbon, hydrogen, oxygen, phosphorus and nitrogen. The particular molecular configuration of DNA in an organism determines the biochemical make-up of all the different types of cells which constitute that organism. DNA is packaged into genes which provide the code for a sequence of amino acids. Each sequence produces a different protein. Genes are packaged into chromosomes each of which is responsible for a different area of protein-building in the organism. Collectively, proteins make up the tissue of the organism and enable it to function. Genes may thus be thought of as the 'words' of the in-built instruction book for the growth and development of the organism. 'Across the entire range of living organisms, the genetic code differs only very slightly, strongly suggesting that all life on Earth may have a common ancestor.'[9] As we shall see, the characteristics of uniformity and simplicity in

---

9   B. and D. Charlesworth, *Evolution, A Very Short Introduction* (Oxford University Press, 2003), p 29.

organic life do undermine a central premise of ID theory – that the complexity and variety of species can be explained only on the basis that they were individually designed and created by God. But it will be argued that uniformity and simplicity, far from undermining it, do provide rational support for the view that God exists and that the existence of God is indicated by the design of organisms.

Genetic Mutation and Natural Selection

The process of reproduction differs from species to species, but the 'variation' which is at the heart of Darwin's theory occurs chiefly in sexual reproduction where the offspring of mating male and female organisms comes into being as a single cell formed by the fusion of two parent cells. The DNA of the offspring cell is a copy of DNA selected from the male and female parent individuals – half from each; thus the DNA of the offspring is a new and unique mixture. The 'copy', or inherited, element explains the similarity between parents and children; the 'new and unique mixture' explains the difference between parents and their children and between siblings.

In the early stages of embryo development, random[10] errors may occur in the copying of the offspring's DNA during cell division and differentiation. These copying errors ('mutations') apart, the process of reproduction would produce offspring all of whose genes were replicas of the selected parental genes. The species would, over time, flourish or decline according to its ability to deal with any changes which occurred in the environment in which the species lives. Genetic mutations are often detrimental to the offspring, and may be manifested by illness or deformity. Occasionally, however, mutations happen to be beneficial.

---

10   See immediately below.

This is when the characteristic governed by the mutation happens to improve the adaptation of the organism to its environment. This means that the individual organism – and its offspring which inherit the mutation – will be better equipped to survive and reproduce than individuals without the mutation. It is unsurprisingly the case that *those individuals better able than others to survive and reproduce do in general survive and reproduce better than those less able*. This is 'natural selection'. By this process the beneficial mutation will come gradually to be a new characteristic of the species. Over a long period, this process of occasional beneficial mutation and consequent natural selection may cause such profound alterations in a population of a species that the population ceases to be able to interbreed with non-mutated members of the species. At this point, a new species is said to have evolved.[11]

Randomness and Chance

The DNA copying errors – mutations – are said to be 'random' in the sense that (as noticed in the previous paragraph) they occur indifferently with respect to whether or not they benefit the individual organism in which they occur.[12] They are 'random' also in the sense that their occurrence is apparently not explicable by reference to any natural pattern or rule, so that it cannot be predicted which mutations will occur when. It cannot be predicted because (as, say, in chaos theory) the contingencies or 'variables' which together cause what happens to happen – in this case, the error in genetic copying – are so numerous and heterogeneous that it is in practical terms impossible to collate them and to see how they operate together to

---

11   See Coyne, chapter 7, explaining why and how speciation occurs.
12   See Coyne, pp 128-9.

produce the result in question. So, crucially, 'random' in this sense does not mean 'causeless' – for a mind with unlimited knowledge and a corresponding power to process it could predict when particular mutations would occur; but, here, 'random' means simply 'unpredictable because of limited knowledge of circumstances'[13]. Likewise, if one says that a particular mutation occurs 'by chance' one would be meaning this – and that the probability of its occurring in any particular case (like the chance of winning the national lottery jackpot on the purchase of a single ticket) is very low.

The randomness of mutations is much cited as evidence against the theological view that each separate species of organism is created by a conscious celestial designer – God. For if the occurrence of a mutation which happens to result in a beneficial adaptation is random, it seems difficult to say that this outcome was pre-planned. Evolution has happened via the chance occurrence of mutations which, as Coyne says, have 'turned out to be useful'[14]. They 'turn out' to be useful because the organism in which the mutation has occurred finds itself better adapted to its environment and thus better placed to survive and to reproduce: this is natural selection.

But in the context of evolution there is a paradox at the heart of the question whether things came to be as they are by chance, or, on the contrary, by design (either natural – the predictable operation of the laws of science and mathematics – or intelligent). The unlikelihood of chance alone being the author of the huge variety of organic life as we know it is commonly expressed by explaining the

13 I.e., 'subjectively unpredictable' – see Essay 1, above, at p 20 on 'objective' and 'subjective' unpredictability.

14 *Ibid.*

astronomic odds against a room full of monkeys, each bashing away randomly at a typewriter, happening to produce even a line of (let alone the entire works of) Shakespeare. Without a cogent natural explanation, other than chance, of the design and variety that we observe in organic life, those who attribute that design to an intelligent designer might reasonably claim to have proved their case[15]. If there is a watch, there is a watch-maker[16] – if the only alternative explanation for the existence of the watch is that a tornado happened to blow through the junkyard and happened to pick up just the right bits for a watch and arrange them in just the right configuration. But, as Dawkins explains in *The Blind Watchmaker*[17], there is a monumental difference in outcome between, on the one hand, the working of random mutation by chance alone and, on the other, the working of random mutation by a process of accumulation:

> **Individual mutations occur randomly** *but the beneficial random mutations necessary to produce an organism which is better than its ancestor at surviving and reproducing (i.e., which has a selective advantage[18] over its ancestor) occur by a process* of **accumulation of mutations** *which massively speeds up the evolutionary process. Dawkins illustrates this with his 'METHINKS IT IS LIKE A WEASEL' computer program. Start with 28 random key strokes (representing the aggregate of letters and spaces in the phrase). Then program the machine to*

15 Cf Essay 1, p 25 above: ' If, then, the choice for explaining fine tuning is between chance and conscious, intelligent, pre-existing being – 'God' – many feel (some reluctantly) that God wins.'

16 William Paley's metaphor in his *Natural Theology* (1802).

17 Chapter 3.

18 The evolutionary advantage derived by an organism from its possession of a characteristic which enables it to survive and reproduce better than other organisms.

*copy this random sequence repeatedly but with a small (e.g. 5%) chance of introducing one error (one 'mutation') in the copying. When via a number of repeated copyings a mutation produces a string of letters nearer to the phrase, begin the process again **with this 'improved' string**. This is in effect how evolution goes – and as Dawkins shows, proceeding in this way from an initial random string to the phrase itself takes some 50 'generations', whereas beginning again and again with a new random sequence would take astronomically longer.*

So, random mutation and natural selection operate cumulatively upon existing life forms to evolve more complex and varied forms of life; upon which *varied forms* random mutation and natural selection operate ... and so on. The speed of cumulatively based selection (compared with that of selection based purely on the chance occurrence of individual mutations) at least makes it possible that things have come to be as they are by cumulative random mutation and natural selection and within the time-frame that the geologists and cosmologists give us.

Now, here is the paradox. The atheist needs to get well away from unimproved or unenhanced chance as the engine of natural order if he is to offer a credible alternative to Paley's 'watchmaker' argument for intelligent design. But the further the atheist goes from unenhanced chance, the closer he comes to law, or principle, or pattern. And the nearer one comes to these concepts as explanations of how things are, the more difficult it becomes to rule out the possibility that if things are happening according to some established pattern, perhaps that pattern existed before things got going; and that a pre-existing pattern may suggest a pre-existing pattern-maker. Which is what the theists are saying. Against this, the theory of cumulative random mutation and natural selection does seem to sail in a good, deep channel between what are, for atheists, the rock of unenhanced chance and the hard place of pre-existing pattern. But is it the case, as Dawkins claims, that 'the evidence of evolution reveals a universe without design'? Does the evidence for evolution by cumulative random mutation and natural selection (CRMNS) show that belief in a God whose existence is indicated by the design of organisms is, at least, overwhelmingly improbable?

'The best theory available'

Before addressing that question, consider first the possibility that evolution by CRMNS is by no means the whole of the story. In the first place, the central question of whether organic life itself can and did evolve from inorganic matter remains unanswered. Then, there are many things that scientists do not know about how evolution works. For example, they cannot currently demonstrate – whether in the laboratory or from the fossil record or by computer simulation – that any particular class of higher animal did evolve, or, within the time[19] and other constraints in question could have evolved, solely by CRMNS. We simply do not know whether it is possible that flying birds, for example, could have evolved solely by CRMNS. The number and combination of mutations required for the formation of the wing is unknown. Also unknown is whether the combination of such mutations could happen by CRMNS alone. It is not difficult to see that there may well be environmental circumstances in which to be able

---

19 Dawkins (*The Blind Watchmaker* (hereafter, *BW*) p 319) accepts that the theory of cumulatively based natural selection can work 'only if there has been sufficient time to fit all the intermediate [stages] in' and states that 'It is the contention of the Darwinian world-view' that this proviso is met. It is a contention which awaits demonstration.

to fly or to glide will confer a selective advantage upon those who can do so. But '…each step of the process, each elaboration of an adaptation, must confer a reproductive benefit on individuals possessing it.'[20] Did natural selection operate alone so as to preserve 'work in progress' until all necessary mutations were in place to permit each of the series of genetic steps required to produce a wing? How much of a selective advantage would have been conferred by the first mutations which (with hindsight) we can see were the initial prerequisites of the development of a wing? Dawkins says that evolution by CRMNS is 'the best theory available'[21]. But it should be remembered that the history of science is littered with theories which in their time were the best available – most recently, Newtonian physics before Planck ushered in Quantum Theory.[22]

Consider next the possibility that, in time, it becomes clearly established that CRMNS is substantially[23] the whole of the story – that it is the governing mechanism operating to produce the world of organisms as we know it. On that basis, we shall then be able to envisage clearly every detail of the course of the history of organic development and to see that, beginning with the primordial soup (or other original crucible of life) CRMNS has been, and continues to be, the chief engine of evolution.

---

20 Coyne, p 130.

21 *BW*, p 317.

22 'In the last quarter of the [nineteenth] century, a young man in Germany contemplating an academic career was warned against going into physics. It would be better to look elsewhere, for physics was at the end of the road, with so little really worthwhile left to do. The young man's name was Max Planck, and fortunately he ignored the advice he had been given.' John Polkinghorne, *Quantum Theory, A Very Short Introduction* (Oxford University Press, 2002), p 4.

23 Cf note 4, above.

But on either of the above two possible accounts of the operation of CRMNS are we still able to say that God created the world in general and species, including *homo sapiens*, in particular? If we did say this, what could we mean?

Intelligence and Design

We could mean that God brought matter into being and designed it to behave as it does.[24] Since he designed it, he knew how it would behave, so he knew that one outcome of organic evolution by cumulatively based natural selection would be intelligent life as exemplified by *homo sapiens*. Does this seem unlikely in the light of the facts as we know them viewed in the light of what we know about evolution? The first question is whether evolution by CRMNS in itself provides an argument against belief in a creator God – as, for example, the depth of undeserved suffering provides an argument[25] against belief in a loving Heavenly Father. The key issue on the evolution question is the complexity of organic life. Paley's 'watchmaker' analogy uses this complexity as the basis of an argument for the existence of a God who created and designed the world of which we are part. If evolution by CRMNS is either the or a governing mechanism producing organic life in all its complexity, it certainly destroys Paley's argument in the form in which he put it. For CRMNS is then a sufficient explanation of that

---

24 Essay 1, above, argues that it may reasonably be thought that there are features of current scientific understanding of the origin and character of the physical universe – in particular of its suitability for the emergence of life, and for the evolution of intelligent beings – which support the belief that the universe is the product of a conscious, intelligent, pre-existing being – 'God'.

25 This 'undeserved suffering argument' for atheism is examined in the Postscript to this book, 'God, Science and Suffering'.

complexity of organic life which Paley used as an argument for intelligent creation in the absence of any alternative argument. But is evolution by CRMNS a *counter*-argument – an argument against belief in a creator God?

There is no basis for arguing that a creator God *could not* have done his work by way of CRMNS evolution. But if we suggest that he did, we do raise questions which a non-evolutionary account of creation does not raise. Take first the question of whether it is plausible to argue that God could have created all the species including *homo sapiens* by way of CRMNS evolution. As we have seen, the chemical formulae, or codes, for the making of all cells of all plant and animal species are contained in DNA molecules composed of just five elements. If evolution by CRMNS is the governing mechanism behind all organic life we can make the following statements:

> [1] that all organic life is produced according to chemical formulae whose building blocks or letters (DNA molecules) are simple and largely uniform across all species;
> [2] that the characteristics of the organisms produced and reproduced according to these formulae change and diversify chiefly through a combination of mutations in DNA and the effect of natural selection upon individuals displaying certain of these mutations.

If, looking back, we can see that this is how things *have happened*, it is possible that an intelligent being foresaw at the start that this is how things *would happen*. We know that organisms mutate and that some mutations will be favoured by natural selection. It is possible that life was created by a God who knew that this would be the case. Now, it is true that our knowledge of how evolution works does not enable us to predict with any precision how things will go in the future. There is too much contingency both within and outside organic life for this to be possible. But it is not nonsensical, nor is it contrary to the evidence we have, to postulate that a God of unlimited cognitive capacity knew and intended that life – fundamentally simple and uniform with its structural basis of DNA – would flourish and diversify; and, in particular, that evolution would in time produce intelligent beings. If this were the case, could not one then say intelligibly that God created the world in general and species, including *homo sapiens*, in particular?

It might be objected that this is 'not the kind of creation' which Christians, for instance, believe in and the Bible portrays. This would be a matter for theologians and biblical scholars. But in the Christian account of the creative relationship between God and any human individual, there is of course a critical element of non-divine agency. For in this account human free will plays a critical part in the (pro)creation of all individuals, though not, certainly, of the human species. Thus, bound as we are in our thought and understanding by what we perceive as dimensions of space and time, it makes no sense to say that God made me or you in the way in which it can be said that I made a table or you a machine. If we have free will, it makes no sense for us to say that God knew how we would exercise it. So it makes no sense to say that God knew what each of us would be before we were conceived by the exercise of their free will by our parents. Similarly, under the theory of evolution by cumulatively based selection, it makes no sense to say that God created humankind as you or I make a table or a machine. But it does make sense to ascribe to God a knowledge of the properties and potential of what he did create.

At the end of *The Blind Watchmaker* Richard Dawkins observes:

> The one thing that makes evolution such a neat theory is that it explains how organized complexity can arise out of primeval simplicity.

> If we want to postulate a deity capable of engineering all the organized complexity in the world, either instantaneously or by guiding evolution, that deity must already have been vastly complex in the first place.[26]

For Dawkins, 'all the organised complexity in the world [of organisms]' comes, via evolution, 'out of primeval simplicity' – whereas any postulated 'deity must already have been vastly complex in the first place'. But indivisible one-ness and simplicity are qualities which theologians attribute to God: the phrase 'primeval simplicity' might be thought an appropriate ascription. May one not think of God as the author of what Dawkins characterises as the primevally simple process in which the chemical codes for the making of all cells of all plant and animal species are contained in DNA molecules composed of just five elements – a process which, through the further natural processes of mutation and selective adaptation, produces organic life in all its complexity?

Whether the evolutionary account of the appearance of *homo sapiens* is or is not in all respects consistent with Christian doctrine may require clarification. At any rate, it does appear possible to view God as having used evolution as his method of creating humankind 'in his own image'[27] as intelligent and morally autonomous beings. Dawkins says that to 'allow [God] some sort of supervisory role over the course that evolution has taken' is 'superfluous'[28]. It is superfluous, in his view, because the theory of evolution is

---

26 *BW*, p 316.
27 Genesis 1:27.
28 *BW, ibid.*

an entirely self-sufficient explanation of how things in the organic world are and came to be. We can grant that there may be no role for God 'within the system'; but Dawkins appears to insist that no questions remain about what is going on 'outside the system'. He is not alone. There is today a powerful current of scientific thought which, in effect, sees the whole course of cosmological 'evolution' rather as Dawkins sees the particular case of organic evolution: that is, as organized complexity arising out of the primeval simplicity of a very few basic physical laws and the laws of logic. And, like Dawkins, some of the proponents of this view assert that it somehow rules out questions about what is going on outside the system with which they are, empirically, dealing. So, a recent television documentary,[29] it was said,

> reveals the science behind much of beauty and structure in the natural world and discovers that far from it being magic or an act of God, it is in fact an intrinsic part of the laws of physics. Amazingly, it turns out that the mathematics of chaos can explain how and why the universe creates exquisite order and pattern.

The thesis appears to be that if the evolution of the universe can be comprehensively understood in terms of physical laws and the laws of logic, this understanding axiomatically answers all the questions about the universe which can intelligibly be asked. On that basis, it is concluded (by Dawkins and others) that the evidence for evolution shows that belief in a God whose existence is indicated by the design of organisms is overwhelmingly improbable. And as the evidence for evolution continues to stack up, the

---

29 *The Secret Life of Chaos,* Jan 2010, BBC 4. The quotation appeared on the BBC 4 website.

improbability becomes more overwhelming. But it is crucial to understand that this claimed improbability is based not so much upon the *strength* but, rather, upon the *nature* of the evidence: the atheist argument is that if the laws of physics and mathematics 'can explain how and why the universe creates exquisite order and pattern', that – axiomatically, without further argument – rules out further rational enquiry. If that axiom can be challenged, the conclusion, of course, no longer follows. Can the axiom be challenged?

II. RATIONAL BELIEF

To accept, as Coyne says, that 'evolution is true' does determine the answer to questions about *how* God may be said to have created species. But it leaves open the question of *whether* God exists and may be said to be, in the words of the Christian Creed, 'creator of all that is'. An affirmative answer to this question is not, indeed cannot be, ruled out by scientific investigation. But may such an answer be said to be 'rational'? A commonly-held view is that only beliefs based on empirical observation are rational, that beliefs which are not empirically verifiable or falsifiable are not rational – they are, instead, 'acts of faith'. On this view, reason and religious faith inhabit different realms: where faith begins, reason ends. Now, certainly, the statement 'I believe that the universe was created by God' is not a statement like 'I believe that all life on Earth has evolved from one primitive species over a period of 3.5 billion years'. The belief in evolution can be subjected to experimental testing. The belief that the universe came to exist through God's creative action cannot be either verified or falsified by experimental observation. It is not a belief about some aspect of what can be verified or falsified by this method. It is, rather, a belief about how what can be verified or falsified in this way came to be. It follows that to show that belief in God is 'rational' it is necessary to show that a belief may be rational even though it is not empirically verifiable. It will be argued here that those who say that only what is empirically verifiable is believable on rational grounds are adopting an approach to rationality which is too narrow. And that the wider approach which emerges from this analysis justifies the contention that a belief may be rational even though it is not empirically verifiable.

The limits of empiricism

The empiricist thesis is, essentially, that *we have reason to believe the evidence of our senses, but if we believe anything else, our belief is not rational: it is an 'act of faith'.* The empiricist may accept that this thesis is itself an act of faith. But he can say that he is happy to confine his attentions to the realm of the rational (of what 'is'), leaving others to explore the realm of faith. The trouble is that those who do wish to explore that realm begin with what they feel instinctively is the disadvantage that all their thoughts are axiomatically non-rational. This is a bee which has been buzzing more or less loudly ever since it was given wings by the eighteenth century empiricist philosopher David Hume who famously wrote:

> If we take in our hand any volume of divinity or school metaphysics, for instance, let us ask, Does it contain any abstract reasoning concerning quantity or number? No. Does it contain any experimental reasoning concerning matter of fact and existence? No. Commit it then to the flames, for it can contain nothing but sophistry and illusion.[30]

---

30 *Inquiry Concerning Human Understanding*, Section XII, Part 3.

What Hume says is that, the laws of mathematics apart, we can know only what is in principle capable of being perceived by the senses and verified by experiment. That is what 'is': that is the universe. Among the mass of things that aren't, are God and reason-based morality – two of Hume's special targets. But here is a fundamental difficulty. Hume's argument is in support of the empiricist thesis, but it is not an empirical argument. Indeed it cannot be: it is bad logic to seek to establish a proposition by relying upon elements of the proposition. So, either all philosophy which considers the bases of knowledge (whether mathematical or empirical) is by definition non-rational (because non-mathematical and non-empirical) or it is not (because 'rational' extends beyond mathematical and empirical). If such philosophy is axiomatically non-rational, we have no more reason for paying attention to Hume (or any other proponent of empiricism) than for ignoring him. Only if such philosophy may be rational may we claim reason for preferring Hume to Aquinas (or any other philosopher arguing for the rationality of belief in God). But if we may claim reason for preferring Hume to Aquinas, we may (both in principle and, if our reasoning is valid, in practice) claim reason for preferring Aquinas to Hume.

Hume would have been unlikely to describe his conclusion as an 'act of faith' and would no doubt have been prepared to concede that his thinking was rational. Similarly, having in 1902 undermined the foundations of Gottlob Frege's attempt to demonstrate the logical impregnability of mathematics, Bertrand Russell spent ten years producing, with A. N. Whitehead, *Principia Mathematica* as an attempt[31] to repair the damage. It

---

31 Unavailing, it seems: see Simon Singh, *Fermat's Last Theorem* (London: Fourth Estate, 1997) ch 4.

seems likely that Russell would have regarded his effort as rational rather than as an act of faith, notwithstanding that it was concerned with establishing foundations for the laws of mathematics rather than with their operation. If Hume's philosophy (or that of other atheist-empiricist philosophers) is rational, what makes it so? It is rational, surely, if and because it provides a defensible answer to the question 'why may one see the universe as simply the product of mathematical and scientific laws?'. But Aquinas's philosophy[32] (and that of other Judeo-Christian philosophers) will be rational too, surely, if and because it provides a defensible answer to the question 'why may one see the universe and the laws which govern it as the creation of a pre-existing, intelligent being?' There may be valid – sound or defensible, well-grounded – reasons for doubting God's existence and valid reasons for affirming it. To deny it or to affirm it, if based on such reasons, would be an act of rational judgement – of balancing competing considerations and reaching a view. To believe in God (as to decline to believe) on the basis of a balancing of competing valid reasons is, quintessentially, a rational process.

Reasons for belief

The central contention of this essay, it will be recalled, is that to believe in God, and to believe that the existence of God is indicated by the design of organisms, are beliefs which may rationally be held. To say of anything that it is designed

---

32 Russell dismissed Aquinas's arguments for the existence of God as 'not philosophy but special pleading' because Aquinas was arguing for what he already believed to be the case. But, as has often been observed, Russell's judgement lies awkwardly in the mouth of one who in *Principia Mathematica* devoted much effort to proving the proposition that 1+1=2. (See Anthony Kenny, *A Brief History of Western Philosophy* (Blackwell Publishers, 1998), p 139.)

means merely that it has a design – a discernible scheme or arrangement which governs its functioning. Organisms in particular and the universe in general are designed in this sense. To say this does not mean necessarily that there is a designer. But it does raise the question. Richard Dawkins and others, as we have seen, take the view that if the design of organisms – and of the universe – can be comprehensively understood in terms of mathematical and scientific laws, that somehow answers the question: there is no designer of the system because the design of the system can be comprehensively understood in terms of the mathematical and scientific laws which govern it.

A two-stage argument against this reasoning has been advanced above. In the section on EVOLUTION AND DESIGN it was argued that even if and when it comes to be demonstrable that the design of organisms in particular and of the universe in general can be comprehensively understood in terms of mathematical and scientific laws, the question of the origin of the universe and the laws remains. Then, in this section on RATIONAL BELIEF, under the heading *The limits of empiricism*, it has been argued that those who say that only what is empirically verifiable is believable on rational grounds are adopting an approach to rationality which is too narrow and that in principle there may be reasons for believing in God which, though not empirically verifiable, are nevertheless valid. But to show this is not, of course, to show that there are actually such reasons. Are there?

Consider the following statements:

1   The earth exists

2   The universe exists

3   God exists

- It is evident that 1 & 2 are alike in being empirically verifiable and that 3 is unlike 1 & 2 in this respect.

- If something can be said to exist it makes sense to ask how it came to exist. As a matter of scientific observation, the earth came to exist through the operation of pre-existent mathematical and scientific laws. As a matter of logic, the universe may have come to exist through the operation of pre-existent mathematical and scientific laws; or through the creative action of a pre-existent, intelligent being – 'God'; or, like God, it may be said to 'simply exist'. If the universe came to exist through the operation of pre-existent mathematical and scientific laws it makes sense to ask how they came to exist. As a matter of logic, they may have come to exist through the creative action of a pre-existent God; or they may simply exist.

- The statements 'the universe simply exists' and 'God simply exists' are alike in that neither is empirically verifiable. The fact that the statement 'the universe exists' is empirically verifiable has no bearing on the verifiability of the statement 'the universe simply exists'. Empirically, the earth clearly exists, but that does not provide any evidence that it simply exists. The same analysis applies to the statement 'pre-existent mathematical and scientific laws simply exist'.

- Atheists advance non-scientific reasons for believing that the universe (or that the laws) simply exist. Theists advance non-scientific reasons for believing that the universe is the creation of a God who simply exists. On the basis, contended for above, that 'rational' extends beyond 'mathematical and empirical', to choose to adopt either of these beliefs may be a rational choice if the reasons for the choice are valid. There is no basis for labelling either of these beliefs intrinsically 'more rational' than the other.

What reasons, then, of a non-scientific sort, may a theist advance for his belief?

As observed above, organisms in particular and the universe in general are designed in the sense that they have a discernible scheme or arrangement which governs their functioning. It might be said that 'design' is a 'feature' or a 'characteristic' of the material world. But, strictly speaking, 'design' is not a feature of the material world in the same sense as atomic or sub-atomic particles or DNA-based organisms are. 'Design' is not a feature *of* the material world. It describes *how we perceive* that world: we, as intelligent beings, perceive it to be arranged according to law or rule. The human mind (in its logical and scientific explorations of what it perceives) 'stamps' the universe with the label 'designed'. Design may be said to be the hallmark of mind in the sense that design is how (the human) mind 'makes sense' of what it perceives.

Mind, then, perceives order in matter. If design is the mind's perception of order, design is, as a perception, the creation of mind. Mind perceives order and is aware that it does so. Without mind there would be no perception of order – no discernment of the scheme or arrangement which governs the functioning of things. Design is order *perceived* by mind; and the human mind asks whether design may not, too, be order *conceived* by a greater mind. It sees that design may be the hallmark of mind not only in the sense that design is how the human mind 'makes sense' of what it perceives but in a more profound sense:

that the human mind perceives the existence of 'mind in matter'[33]. That perception may be expressed by saying that the material universe is the product of a pre-existing mind – or, in conventional terms, that the material universe comes to exist through the agency of a pre-existent, intelligent being – 'God'. Since this statement is nothing other than a reasoned reflection upon the perception of design (the design of the universe in general and of organisms in particular) it may be taken as a reasoned, or rational, basis for belief in God, and for belief that the existence of God is indicated by the design of the universe in general and of organisms in particular.

This is a rational judgement of a rational being about the origin and nature of the rational universe of which that being is a part. The judgement is rational in the sense just explained. The being who makes it is rational in the sense that he or she is endowed with the faculty of reason – with intelligence – and uses that faculty to make the judgement. The universe is rational in the sense that it behaves in a manner which is governed by mathematical and scientific laws. Any religion which bases its beliefs upon these considerations is rationally based. A foundational text of the Christian religion is the opening passage of St John's gospel: 'In the beginning was the Word, ... and the Word was God.... [A]ll things were made through him'. Christianity is thus a religion which takes as its rational base the belief that the material universe came to exist through the agency of a pre-existent, intelligent being – God or 'the Word' – in Greek, *logos*.

---

33 Theistic and atheistic versions of the belief that mind is the fundamental characteristic of the world are the subject of Essay 3 below.

To say that a religion is rationally based is not, of course, to claim that reason compels belief. Nor is it to say that all individuals' acts of belief are necessarily based upon rational considerations; or that those which are based upon rational considerations are exclusively so based. But it is to insist that, if one believes, one's act of faith may be also an act of reason.

3. Consciousness

Aim Without Intention? –
Reflections on Thomas Nagel's
Mind and Cosmos[1]

In tackling the problem of why and how consciousness arose on earth, a primary issue is whether it is 'just a local problem [about] the relation between mind, brain and behavior in living animal organisms'[2]; or whether, on the contrary, it is a problem about the fundamental nature of the universe which, therefore, 'invades our understanding of the entire cosmos and its history'[3].

The 'local' approach to the problem is commonly encountered as part of a materialist-atheist world view which runs roughly as follows. All that occurs – everything that is the case – can in principle be fully explained by the 'natural sciences' as that term is currently understood. Consciousness is a feature of animal behaviour which can in principle (and may in due course in fact) be fully understood in purely neuro-physiological terms: consciousness is nothing more than a feature of certain brain states, just as liquidity is simply a feature of the arrangement of atoms of hydrogen and oxygen which we call water.[4] Contrastingly, in what may be labelled the 'universal' approach,

---

1 Thomas Nagel, *Mind and Cosmos: Why the Materialist Neo-Darwinian Conception of Nature is Almost Certainly False* (Oxford: Oxford University Press, 2012; hereafter, *Nagel*).

2 *Nagel,* p 3.

3 *Ibid.*

4 But cf discussion in *Nagel* at pp 40-1, 56; and in Galen Strawson et al., *Consciousness and its Place in Nature – Does Physicalism Entail Panpsychism?* (Exeter: Imprint Academic, 2006) p 13.

consciousness is very much more than simply a feature of certain brain states. It is seen as a manifestation of 'mind' which is either *a* or *the* fundamental characteristic of the world – a characteristic strikingly displayed in the world's intelligibility and in the existence of conscious beings with the capacity to understand to some degree the world of which they are part. The view that mind is *the* fundamental characteristic is most familiarly encountered as part of a theistic world view. Theism sees the emergence of conscious organisms and, more specifically, the emergence of human beings, whose consciousness extends to great powers of both intellect and evaluative judgement, as reflecting the intention of a supernatural, conscious, intelligent being – 'God' – in causing the universe to be as it is.

In *Mind and Cosmos*, Thomas Nagel offers a world view occupying what he describes as 'the territory between'[5] materialism and theism. This territory he sees as neither including the supernatural of theism nor confined to the 'brute matter'[6] of materialism. It is occupied, rather, by a natural world of which mind is 'a[7] basic aspect ... [and] the intelligibility of the world, as described by the laws that science has uncovered, is itself part of the deepest explanation of why things are as they are'[8]; also of how conscious beings – to whom the world's intelligibility is manifest – have appeared. Nagel's world view is thus universal but atheistic; naturalistic but not materialist. It may be described as a kind of mental-physical, or 'psychophysical'[9], naturalism.

---

5   *Nagel*, p 22.
6   I.e., matter 'not possessing or connected with reason, intelligence, or sensation; ... merely material' (*OED*).
7   A basic aspect, together with the physical, rather than *the* basic aspect as in theism.
8   *Nagel*, pp 16-17.
9   *Ibid*, p 50.

Psychophysical naturalism is a type of world view much less commonly encountered (whether in scholarly or in everyday thinking) than either materialism or theism. These, indeed, are popularly regarded as the only two seriously arguable positions. But in fact, as will appear below, psychophysical naturalism has not only a considerable pedigree but also a substantial place in contemporary thought. This essay focuses upon Nagel's book since it is a penetrating (whether or not successful) recent attempt to elaborate the case for this third, 'middle-ground', type of world view which sees 'mind' as fundamental in a wholly natural world.

In Part I of this essay some account will be given of materialism and theism and of the reasons why psychophysical naturalists find both implausible as world views: materialism because it sees mind as an 'add-on'[10] rather than as a basic aspect of nature; theism because it sees mind as pre-existing the natural world rather than as a basic aspect of it. Part II will examine the chief features of psychophysical naturalism. All forms of naturalism definitionally exclude the notion of mind conceived of as a seat of consciousness distinct from, and pre-existing, the natural world. The view that mind is fundamental in a naturalistic cosmos means that mind is conceived of as governing the origin and development of that cosmos but as somehow a part of it, and not, like the God of theism, distinct from it. In this ('teleological'[11]) view, originating mind can impart a direction or goal to the unfolding of the cosmos but without there being any pre-existing, conscious mind whose intention sets that goal. In Part III the essay will conclude with a discussion of this notion of goal, or aim, without intention.

---

10   *Ibid*, p 16.
11   See Part II, below.

I. MATERIALISM AND THEISM

Materialism

Materialism is 'the theory ... that nothing exists except matter[12] and ... that mental phenomena are nothing more than, or are wholly caused by, the operation of material or physical agencies'[13].

For the psychophysical naturalist, materialism is implausible essentially because it takes for granted (as not requiring special explanation), firstly, the orderliness in matter – the intelligibility of its behaviour – which empirical science reveals and, secondly, the emergence of conscious, intelligent beings such as ourselves. The psychophysical naturalist, on the contrary, sees both as revealing a primal mental quality in the natural world – a quality which explains not only the intelligibility of the world but also the emergence of intelligent beings within it.

What account do materialists give of the emergence of consciousness and other mental phenomena such as cognition – the acquisition of knowledge by a conscious being[14] through perception, reflection and reasoning – and evaluative judgement? Essentially they lump them in with everything else. Physics, chemistry and biology approach ever nearer to yielding what has passed into common parlance as a 'theory of everything'. Humankind's immense and ever-growing knowledge of what matter is

---

12 Or, rather, perhaps, '"physical stuff" ... because "matter" is now specially associated with mass although energy is just as much in question, as indeed is anything else that can be said to be physical, e.g. spacetime....' Strawson, *op cit*, p 3 note 1.

13 *OED.*

14 I follow Nagel in assuming 'that the attribution of knowledge to a computer is a metaphor and that the higher-level cognitive capacities can be possessed only by a being that also has consciousness ....' *Nagel*, p 71.

and how it behaves, yields an account of cosmological events from a beginning some 13.7 billion years ago to the present and the likely future. The account explains in terms of physics and chemistry the material developments (from the 'Big Bang' to the formation of atoms, galaxies, stars and planets) which occurred prior to the emergence of life and, in the same terms, explains the chemistry of biogenesis. Materialism sees this development of inorganic matter as the fortuitously well-ordered outcome of the random[15] workings of cause and effect. Then comes evolution which explains the subsequent history of life in terms of random[16] genetic mutation and natural selection. Consciousness appears well down the evolutionary road and, according to materialists, must be accounted for in the same basic way. But too much hangs on that 'must'. For, as Nagel observes:

> If we continue to assume that we are parts of the physical world and that the evolutionary process that brought us into existence is part of its history, then something must be added to the physical conception of the natural order that allows us to explain how it can give rise to organisms that are more than physical.... The appearance of animal consciousness is evidently the result of biological evolution, but this well-supported empirical fact is not yet an explanation.[17] *[For, as he remarks earlier:]* Merely to identify a cause is not to provide a significant explanation, without some understanding of why the cause produces the effect.[18]

---

15 'Random' here means unpredictable because of limited knowledge of circumstances (see further, next note). Some materialists overcome the implausibility of a randomness-based analysis by re-situating their world view on what many find the far less plausible ground of multiverse theory: see Essay 1, above, p 27.

16 See *Randomness and Chance* in Essay 2, above, p 38.

17 *Nagel,* p 46.

18 *Ibid,* p 45.

Plainly, then, Nagel's quarrel is not with the Darwinian theory of organic development through replication with variation and selection – but with materialism – the view that matter and its behaviour (including evolution) are to be understood purely mechanistically, and in particular that consciousness is nothing more than a feature of certain brain states.

Materialism, of course, is not a scientific theory capable of verification or falsification by empirical observation. It is, rather, (like psychophysical naturalism) a metaphysical theory about the natural world and science: matter is all that exists; the nature and behaviour of matter is the province of science, so science can tell us all there is to know about matter – and, therefore, about all that exists[19]. Thus the fact that matter behaves according to discoverable ('scientific') laws is fundamental to our understanding of the origin and nature of the cosmos; but the fact that there are such laws and that in certain circumstances matter configures itself in a form – e.g. the human brain – through which it becomes aware of itself and of those laws neither requires nor is capable of further explanation. How plausible is this theory?

Understanding the formation and properties of non-organic matter purely in terms of the laws of physics and chemistry may seem, to some, intuitively plausible; likewise, possibly, the chemical processes which appear to have produced simple life forms from non-organic matter.[20] And also, perhaps, (given the emergence of life) it may be

---

19 The claim that science is the exclusive source of knowledge is a variety of materialism known as 'scientism' (see Preface, above).

20 Although, as Nagel notes (p 6), 'There is much … uncertainty in the scientific community about … the likelihood that self-reproducing life forms should have come into existence spontaneously on the early earth, solely through the operation of the laws of physics and chemistry.'

intuitively plausible to see the evolution of sophisticated life forms purely in terms of random mutation and natural selection. All these processes may seem, intuitively, purely material, purely physical. But how much more territory can these foundational intuitions of materialism plausibly be said to cover?

Firstly, the operation and interaction of the various natural forces (gravity, electromagnetism and the nuclear forces), to say nothing of the quantum-to-classical transition, which together produce a 'finely tuned' universe 'just right for life'[21], seem to many to display a quality of orderliness, of intelligibility, which cannot plausibly be treated as requiring no explanation beyond the purely material. Moreover, and critically in assessing the plausibility of the neo-Darwinian materialist account of evolution, experience – consciousness – seems intuitively of a different order from the purely material. To be sure, the way in which organisms respond to light, sound and proximity to other material phenomena may be reducible to purely material terms.[22] But experience – the 'inner point of view'[23] – is, intuitively, of a different order – 'real' but not material. A purely material account of whatever it is which has experience contains no account of experience itself – of *what it is like to be*[24] that which has the experience. It is in its failure to offer any explanation of either intelligibility or of experience that, for those who reject materialism, its implausibility as a comprehensive world view lies.

21 See, e.g., Paul Davies, *The Goldilocks Enigma – Why is the Universe Just Right for Life?* (London: Penguin Books, 2007), Martin Rees, *Just Six Numbers* (London: Phoenix, 2000) – both discussed in Essay 1, above.

22 See further, text to note 30, below.

23 *Nagel*, p 38.

24 Cf Nagel's 'What Is It Like to Be a Bat?', *Philosophical Review* LXXXIII (1974), p 435.

For those many who do not share the materialist's belief, its chief shortcoming is its refusal to concede that it may be that the laws of physical science provide only a partial account of why things are as they are – its refusal to concede that it may be, on the contrary, that those laws themselves are underwritten and explained by the quality of intelligibility in the behaviour of matter which they reveal; and that this intelligibility, together with the propensity of matter to become conscious of itself and of its intelligibility, must be incorporated into any plausible theory of the origin and nature of the cosmos.

Theism

Theism, certainly, does offer an explanation both of the intelligibility of the world and of the emergence of consciousness in it. God is conceived of as a conscious, intelligent being who pre-exists and, by divine creative power, wills into existence the physical universe of space and time. Human and such other kinds of conscious, intelligent beings as there may be in this physical universe are conceived of as intended by God to come into existence within and as part of the physical universe. So it is, on the one hand, the capacities of consciousness, intelligence and creative power attributed to God which are held to explain the origin and nature of the physical universe: the intelligible, orderly, behaviour of brute matter is explained by the pre-existence of creative mind which intends these qualities of intelligibility and orderliness to characterise its creation. And it is, on the other hand, the capacities of consciousness and intelligence in human beings (and such other conscious, intelligent beings as there may be) which are explained by what is conceived of as a divine sense of purpose – to share with divine creation the very qualities of consciousness and intelligence which are fundamental qualities of the divinity. Further, many who take a theistic world view see the divine sense of purpose in which they believe as both benevolent and beneficent. This is essentially how theists experience value – goodness – as part of the created universe: the goodness of life is as fundamental a feature of the cosmos as its intelligibility and as the existence of conscious beings with cognitive capacity. To be sure, many, perhaps most, human beings, whether theists or not, judge their existence in an intelligible world – and the consciousness and cognitive faculties which reveal that world – to be a good for them. But for the materialist, value, like intelligibility and consciousness, is entirely adventitious.

For Nagel, theism is no more plausible – no more credible – a world view than materialism.[25] Materialism is, for the psychophysical naturalist, not credible because it takes intelligibility and consciousness for granted – as not requiring special explanation. Theism, on the other hand, does explain intelligibility but in a way which the psychophysical naturalist finds also not credible. Nagel admits that he has an 'ungrounded intellectual preference'[26] in favour of naturalism and against belief in God. This is, at least in part, it appears, because theism does not solve the problem of evil which, he says,[27] it poses. But essentially theism is unbelievable for him simply because he does not believe it: he lacks any *sensus divinitatis*.[28] Instead, he takes the 'ungrounded' view that the intelligibility of the world is not to be explained in terms of divine design,

---

25 *Nagel*, p 22.

26 *Ibid*, p 26.

27 *Ibid*, p 25. For a theistic response to the atheist 'undeserved suffering argument', see Postscript, below.

28 *Ibid*, p 12.

divine intention. He accepts that theism can provide 'a comprehensive account of the natural order'[29]. But that is not the type of comprehensive *natural* account which he is seeking.

II. PSYCHOPHYSICAL NATURALISM

The 'primal stuff' and the 'inner point of view'

On any naturalistic world view it is clear that whatever is the primal, or original, stuff of the universe has the capacity to – can in time – produce a world which contains conscious living beings. This is clear simply because it is in fact what has happened. What is not clear is whether this capacity can plausibly be attributed to a primal stuff which is conceived of as being purely physical – brute matter.

Materialists find no difficulty in viewing the universe as having developed over time from a purely physical primal stuff – consisting of fundamental particles and forces – into an increasingly complex and varied world of non-organic matter from which, by a chemical process of abiogenesis, basic life forms eventually emerged. Thereafter, life is seen as having evolved via random genetic mutation and natural selection. And, if one is focusing on the emergence of conscious organisms, it is possible to envisage in purely physical terms the development of brains having all the physical features associated with the notion of consciousness.[30] These features would include reacting appropriately (i.e., beneficially to the organism in question) to light or heat or sound; processing and reacting appropriately to information relating, on the

---

29 *Ibid*, p 26.

30 David Chalmers, *The Character of Consciousness* (Oxford: Oxford University Press, 2010) p 4. These features he calls 'neural correlates of consciousness'.

one hand, to the organism's internal state and, on the other, to its external environment – e.g., needing food and distinguishing food from non-food; having memory (in the computer sense of a function analogous to that of the human faculty of memory) and accessing it appropriately. But such phenomena of information processing neither entail nor explain the occurrence of experience. Machines – computers and some others – can perform such functions but apparently have no experience. There are, also, many organisms which can perform these functions but which apparently, likewise, have no experience. The performance of these functions in these contexts can be fully explained by reference to the physical structure of the machine or organism in question. What cannot be so explained (*pace* the materialists) is the association, in conscious organisms, of these structures and functions with *experience* – an 'inner point of view'[31].

As observed in Part I above, whether materialism can accommodate, if not explain, the occurrence of experience is a metaphysical question whose answer rests ultimately upon individual conviction. Both the psychophysical naturalist and the theist believe that it cannot. For the former, unlike the latter, the explanation of consciousness is, axiomatically, to be found in the natural world; and the natural world is conceived of as a world which has developed in certain ways over time from some form of primal stuff. So far, as with the materialist. But the psychophysical naturalist and the materialist part company in their respective convictions about the nature of the primal stuff. The materialist believes that the primal stuff is purely physical; the psychophysical naturalist believes that it has also a mental quality, meaning that *a comprehensive*

---

31 *Nagel*, p 38, *passim*.

description of the natural properties of this primal stuff will include not only its physical properties but also mental properties[32] which explain the capacity of the primal stuff to configure itself in a form – e.g. the human brain – through which it becomes conscious of itself and of the orderliness of the universe of which it is part.

How is this latter belief articulated?

Mental and physical qualities of the primal stuff: 'neutral monism'

As noted above, there is a long-established train of naturalist/atheist thought based on the conviction that mind is a fundamental feature of the natural world. Both historically and today this train of thought has manifested itself in a wide variety of different theories, but a generic label which captures the essence of many of these theories is 'neutral monism'. Essentially, neutral monism sees the primal stuff of the universe as neither physical nor mental (so, 'neutral') but as embodying (as an indivisible unity – 'monistically') both physical and mental properties. The label 'neutral monism' was first used early in the last century – to describe the thought of Ernst Mach, William James and Bertrand Russell but similar views have been attributed to earlier philosophers, including Hume and Spinoza.

Russell expressed his view thus:

> The stuff of which the world of our experience is composed is … neither mind nor matter, but something more primitive than either. Both mind and matter seem to be composite, and the stuff of which they are compounded lies in a sense between the two, in a sense above them both, like a common ancestor.[33]

---

32 What Nagel calls 'protopsychic properties' (p 66) or 'protomental features of the basic constituents' (p 63).

33 Bertrand Russell, *The Analysis of Mind* (London: George Allen & Unwin, 1921) p 8.

'James's view', Russell wrote, 'is that the raw material out of which the world is built up is not of two sorts, one matter and the other mind, but that it is arranged in different patterns by its inter-relations, and that some arrangements may be called mental, while others may be called physical'[34]. And Mach used colour and our perception of it to illustrate the notion that the primal neutral stuff manifests itself according to its 'inter-relations':

> While a given element is, intrinsically, neither mental nor physical, the various groups to which it belongs may display functional relationships that are characteristic of physics or of psychology. In this case the neutral element forms part of the subject matter of physics and of psychology.... A single neutral element—the color—gets to be both the physical color of a physical object and our mental perception/sensation of it. The color can be called physical, *qua* constituent of the one group, and mental (a sensation), *qua* constituent of the other group, but is the same unchanging and intrinsically neutral element that figures in these two different contexts.[35]

The basic tenet of neutral monism, then, is that the primal stuff of our universe has both a physical and a mental quality – a propensity to both physical and mental manifestations.

Neutral monism retains contemporary support – Nagel, for example, thinks that 'the weight of evidence favors some form of neutral monism'[36] – which, later, he describes as 'a form of panpsychism'[37] whose essence is succinctly captured as follows by Peter Simons.[38]

---

34   *Ibid*, p 17.
35   *Stanford Encyclopedia of Philosophy*, article on *Neutral Monism*.
36   *Nagel*, p 5.
37   *Ibid*, p 57. David Chalmers, *op cit*, p 4.
38   In a sceptical essay in Strawson [a staunch panpsychist] *op cit*, p 146.

(1)   We cannot deny the existence of experience.

(2)   Experience appears to emerge from physical phenomena that are not themselves experiential.

(3)   Wholly non-experiential phenomena are not by their physical nature capable of giving rise to experience.

...

(9)   But all phenomena are physical (Physicalism).

(10)   Therefore all [physical] phenomena are in some way experiential (Panpsychism).

The argument for neutral monism/panpsychism may have force for those who find both materialism and theism implausible as world views. But the difficulty is, as Nagel accepts, that

> the protopsychic properties of matter are postulated solely because they are needed to explain the appearance of consciousness at high levels of organic complexity. Apart from that, nothing is known about them: they are completely indescribable and have no predictable local effects, in contrast to the physical properties of electrons and protons, which allow them to be detected individually.[39]

The history of the universe – causation or teleology?

If the protopsychic properties of the neutral monist's primal stuff are obscure to the point of indescribability, may light perhaps be shed by considering what may be taken to be their consequences? – is it possible to suggest how those properties (whatever they are) may have manifested themselves historically?

---

39 *Nagel*, pp 61-2; also 57-8.

Nagel considers principally the possibility of both 'causative' and 'teleological' historical accounts.[40] In the causative account, the emergence of consciousness is seen as a serendipitous outcome of purely material cause and effect; in the teleological account it is seen as a goal at which the mental quality of the primal stuff is aimed.

The causative account would say that whatever has happened since the Big Bang, including the appearance (on earth or wherever else) of conscious beings, is explained solely by 'the nonteleological and timeless laws of physics'[41]. But Nagel's view[42] is that, the operation over time of a psychophysical causality on the primal stuff is no more describable or imaginable than the protopsychic properties themselves of that primal stuff – except to postulate that the unfolding history of primordial matter is somehow inherent in its intrinsic properties. The fundamental question remains unanswered: 'Why should those properties make the appearance of [conscious] organisms, starting from inorganic matter, at all likely?'[43]

The teleological account, by contrast, would say that whatever has happened, including the appearance on earth, or wherever, of conscious beings, is explained not only by nonteleological and timeless laws of physics but also by 'principles of self-organisation or of the development of complexity over time that are not explained by those elemental laws'[44]. As Nagel later explains, a critical feature of this idea of natural teleology is that 'some laws of nature

---

40 He refers briefly also (p 66) to the theistic intention-based account which, of course, is not an option for a psychophysical naturalistic analysis. On intention, see part III of this essay.

41 *Ibid*, p 92.

42 See *ibid*, pp 63-5.

43 *Ibid*, p 65.

44 *Ibid*, p 59.

would apply directly to the relation between the present and the future, rather than specifying functions that hold at all times'[45]. Is there any contemporary body of thought which may be taken to indicate that there are indeed scientific laws which 'apply directly to the relation between the present and the future' – laws, that is to say, of natural teleology?

Quantum mechanics and natural teleology

In invoking natural teleology in this context one would be focusing upon the primal stuff of which everything else is constituted and seeking to show that there is something intrinsic in that stuff which channels or guides its future development towards the appearance of conscious beings in the world. In recent years it has been suggested that quantum mechanics may support the radically counter-intuitive idea that there is in the primal stuff something intrinsic of this sort *which owes its own existence to the very consciousness whose appearance that intrinsic 'something' is said to explain.* In short, it has been suggested that consciousness, which is generally thought of as a late outcome of the course of events since the Big Bang, may actually have contributed to shaping certain characteristics of the primal stuff from which in the course of time consciousness was bound to, and did, emerge.

The foundation of the apparently fanciful idea that the past may to some degree have been shaped by the future is the central and well-established tenet of quantum mechanics that quantum entities exist ordinarily in a state of 'superposition' – they are, at any given moment, neither exclusively here nor exclusively there: they are, although indivisible, in a sense both here and there. The notion of

45 *Ibid*, p 93.

superposition is dramatically illustrated by the so-called 'two slits experiment' described earlier[46]. In this experiment, a stream of single photons (or other quantum particles, e.g. electrons) is fired towards a screen in which there are two well-separated slits through which the photons can pass. Some distance beyond the slit screen is a detector screen which records the impact of the photons which have passed through the slit screen. Since photons are indivisible, one would expect that each photon which passes through the slit screen would pass through one slit or the other. And if a detector is placed near each slit, then this is indeed what is observed. But if the photons are left unobserved until they hit the more distant detector screen, the record of their impact shows that each indivisible photon passed through both slits, contributing to the build-up of a wave-like pattern on the screen. The process of observation thus seems to determine the behaviour (as either particle or wave) of the photons.

In his book *The Goldilocks Enigma*[47] Paul Davies explains how a refinement of the two slits experiment suggests that the process of observation which apparently determines quantum behaviour may operate in some sense 'backwards' in time. In this 'delayed choice' experiment (first envisaged by the eminent American physicist J. A. Wheeler and later performed in the laboratory with Wheeler's anticipated result) the detector screen of the two slits experiment is replaced by a venetian blind behind which are placed two detectors, each focused upon one of the slit screen slits. A stream of single photons is fired as in the original experiment but the venetian blind is left closed until after a photon has passed through the slit screen. The

---

46   See Essay 1, above, p 18.
47   Above, note 21, at pp 277-80.

experimenter then decides, before the photon has reached the blind, whether to leave the blind closed or to open it. If the blind is left closed, the arrival of the photon is recorded as contributing (as in the original experiment where the photons are left unobserved) to a build-up of a wave pattern. But if the blind is opened after the photon has passed through the slit screen but before it has reached the blind, and the photon is observed by one of the detectors, it will be seen to have passed, particle-like, only through the slit on which that detector was focused. Plainly, then, although the observer decides *after* the photon has passed through the slit screen to open the blind or to leave it closed, that decision determines what happens (i.e., how the photon behaves at the slit screen) *before* it is made. What is the significance of the delayed choice experiment?

- The experiment shows that something happening now (observation of a photon which has recently passed through a slit screen) can shape something which happened previously (the photon passing as a particle through one of two slits rather than as a wave passing through both).

- If it is a general principle of quantum mechanics that observation after an event may contribute to shaping that event as it (previously) happened, then what happened, say, in the early universe may to some degree be shaped by later observation.

- But our knowledge of the natural world indicates that the way things are in the present is the result of the way things were previously.

- So it is apparently conceivable both that, on the one hand, observations in the present of past events (e.g. the development of the early universe) contribute to shaping those past events; and that, on the other, the present state of things, including the existence of conscious observers, is not only a necessary pre-condition for the past events but also their necessary outcome.

- To speak of the existence of conscious observers as a 'necessary outcome' of the quantum behaviour of what is taken to be the primal stuff is to speak teleologically: for it is to suggest that there is something intrinsic in that stuff which channels or guides its future development towards the evolution of conscious beings. And the hypothesis is that the propensity of the primal stuff to generate conscious observers depends upon the quantum effect on the primal stuff of future observation by such observers.

- What is being postulated is a 'causal loop': 'Conventional science assumes a linear logical sequence: cosmos → life → mind. Wheeler suggested closing this chain into a loop: cosmos → life → mind → cosmos'[48.]

As Davies observes,[49] 'It is a huge leap from the delayed-choice experiment, which deals with single photons, to the *entire* universe being somehow created (or at least projected into a definite, concrete form) by its own observer-participators'. Nevertheless, Wheeler's delayed choice experiment does suggest 'the possibility of observers today, and in the future, shaping the nature of physical reality *in the past*, including the far past when no observers existed. That is indeed a radical idea, for it gives life and mind a type of creative role in physics, making them an indispensable part of the entire cosmological story'[50].

---

48 Davies, *ibid*, p 281; see also pp 284-87.
49 *Ibid*, p 282.
50 *Ibid*, p 281.

Can natural teleology explain consciousness?

The proposition ('P') which emerges from the above is that *conscious minds in the present can somehow contribute to the shape of things in the past and so to the manner of their subsequent evolution.* If P can be shown to be true it will follow that conscious mind is a fundamental feature of the natural world. Also, and critically for the psychophysical naturalist theory which Nagel is advancing, P, if true, *explains* why consciousness emerges from the primal stuff: it is because the primal stuff has, as the neutral monists and the panpsychists contend, a mental as well as a physical quality. Moreover, from the psychophysical naturalist's point of view it does not detract from the explanatory power of P that P leaves unanswered the question why 'mind' – the mental quality in the primal stuff – exists. For it is not taken by theists to detract from the explanatory power of theistic belief that it leaves unanswered the question why God exists; nor by materialists to detract from the explanatory power of the materialist thesis that it leaves unanswered the question why matter, or 'physical stuff' exists. Naturalist and theist alike can invoke the aphorism, which had it not been penned by Wittgenstein[51] might be thought a truism, that all explanations end somewhere.

As a proposition claiming scientific support, P is based upon the so-called Copenhagen interpretation of quantum mechanics – the first of a number of radically different interpretations which have been advanced over the last century. As appears from the above, the interpretation allocates a fundamental constitutive role to 'observers'. Whether P is true turns upon whether this aspect of the Copenhagen interpretation is correct. The interpretation held sway among theoretical physicists for half a century

---

51 *Philosophical Investigations*, I, i.

and is still regarded by some in that community as 'orthodox contemporary physics'[52], but it is today, as Davies makes clear,[53] a minority view. Were it correct, it could certainly be said to provide some empirical evidence of teleological natural laws of the kind which Nagel's psychophysical analysis requires in order to give plausibility to the neutral monist theory which he advocates. At any rate, the currency which the view has enjoyed shows that the teleological approach cannot be dismissed as manifestly 'unscientific'.

The fundamental point is that quantum physics, unlike the Newtonian physics whose foundational status it has appropriated, does open the scientific door to a teleological explanation of the appearance of consciousness on earth.

Teleology and cognition

If there are teleological natural laws which explain the appearance of consciousness, they may also, and *a fortiori*, explain cognition – the acquisition of knowledge by a conscious being[54] through perception, reflection and reasoning. In the causal loop 'cosmos → life → mind → cosmos'[55] may 'mind' plausibly be supposed to extend beyond mere consciousness and to include knowledge and understanding? Perhaps, as Davies remarks, '... a universe cannot create and explain itself without also understanding itself'[56].

Furthermore, teleological natural laws, if they exist, might be said not only to explain the appearance of

---

52   Henry Stapp, a theoretical physicist at Berkeley, quoted in
     Strawson, *op cit*, at p 165, and referring to the role in that
     orthodoxy of '*conscious choices* made by human experimenters'.

53   Davies, *op cit*, p 291.

54   See above, note 14.

55   Davies, *op cit*, p 281 (see text to note 48 above).

56   *Ibid*, p 289, *passim*.

consciousness and cognition but also, Nagel suggests,[57] to provide a basis for the belief that human cognitive faculties can yield true knowledge and understanding of the universe. This argument, if accepted, further underpins the view[58] that mind is a fundamental characteristic of the world and at the same time further undermines the contrary neo-Darwinian materialist view.[59] The argument is in essence as follows.

In the neo-Darwinian materialist narrative, cognition, like consciousness, is an evolved characteristic sufficiently explained by random genetic mutation and the selective advantage which it confers upon those organisms which acquire it. But the knowledge we obtain through our cognitive capacity has a quintessential quality which cannot plausibly be explained by reference to selective advantage. That quality is a *certainty* which is derived from our ability to reflect upon the reliability or truthfulness of categories of things that we know. Our conviction, for instance, that particular types of behaviour will be to our advantage in the evolutionary race is derived not from the fact that it is so but from the fact that we know that it is so (a knowing which opens to us a world of further knowledge) – for a correct rational inference is '[a] direct apprehension of the truth ... grasped as valid in itself'[60].

This central feature of our cognitive faculty, like the appearance of consciousness, can be plausibly explained on a teleological basis: that is to say, on the basis that there is a

---

57 *Nagel,* Chapter 4, *Cognition.*

58 See p 62, above.

59 In Chapter 5, *Value,* Nagel argues that this teleological approach may also justify belief in the human capacity to make true judgements of value, a belief which, again, neo-Darwinian materialism rejects.

60 *Nagel,* pp 80-81.

mental quality in the primal stuff which is geared towards the emergence of conscious beings with cognitive capacity. But the materialist narrative based on the random workings of cause and effect cannot plausibly explain the appearance of this central feature of cognition: our certainty that what is so is so. It is not that this certainty – this second level of knowledge, the knowing that one knows – may not be selectively advantageous. It is, rather, that it is radically implausible to attribute having such knowledge to purely material causes. Moreover, the truth of a rational inference cannot be confirmed by the thought that its reliability reflects the selective advantage which that reliability confers:

> I cannot pull back from a logical inference and reconfirm it with the reflection that the reliability of my logical thought processes is consistent with the hypothesis that evolution has selected them for accuracy. That would drastically weaken the logical claim.... [A]ny evolutionary account of the place of reason presupposes reason's validity and cannot confirm it without circularity.... It is not enough to be able to think that *if* there are logical truths, natural selection might very well have given me the capacity to recognize them.[61]

As is apparent, Nagel's argument on cognition depends upon the belief that our reasoning faculty does give us access to real truth about our real world. But as he observes, 'There would be something strange to the point of incoherence about taking scientific naturalism as the ground for antirealism about natural science'[62].

* * *

---

61 *Ibid.*
62 *Ibid*, p 75.

Summary on psychophysical naturalism

The psychophysical naturalist world view discussed above, like the world view of the materialist, seeks to explain the way things are now (and are expected to be in the future) by reference to how they were at the start – to explain the complexity of the universe as a whole in terms of the relative simplicity of what are taken to be its basic elements. The materialist's conviction that the universe, like its primal stuff, is purely physical leads to the view that mental manifestations – consciousness, intelligibility, understanding – somehow emerge from the purely material. The psychophysical naturalist points out that the materialist's view entails either that the mental is in some apparently contradictory sense physical or that the mental emerges somehow magically from the physical. Faced with the unpalatable alternatives of contradiction or magic the psychophysical naturalist postulates that the primal stuff has both a mental and a physical quality. The difficulty of saying anything more about the mental quality than to hypothesise that it exists leads to an exploration of the teleological thesis – the thesis that it is the mental quality of the primal stuff which explains why consciousness and cognition in due course appear in the world. This philosophical thesis may claim support from a central feature of contemporary natural scientific thought. For while natural teleology seems to be ruled out by classical Newtonian physics, there are clear indications that quantum theory may open the door to a teleological analysis.

III. AIM WITHOUT INTENTION?

The nature of the question

Psychophysical naturalism sees 'mind' as a fundamental characteristic of the world. The theory, in its neutral monist form, postulates that the primal stuff of the world has both a mental and a physical quality; and that the mental quality is manifested in natural laws geared to or aimed at – and thus explaining – the appearance of consciousness. But that 'aim' is seen as simply intrinsic to the laws. It is not attributable to the intention of any law maker. From a naturalist perspective there is no law maker, so there can be no intention. The question is whether this notion of 'aim without intention' is coherent – whether, as Nagel himself asks, it 'makes sense'[63].

Usually, the word 'aim' is used to describe human action done with the intention of producing a certain result. But it can make linguistic sense to speak of 'aim' in circumstances where there is no implication of intention. The *Oxford English Dictionary* has examples of such usage: comets, for example, are referred to as 'aiming towards the west'; and, in another example, it is said of a poorly-secured car headlamp that 'the aim of the beam was wrong'. In these examples, the aim of comet and of headlamp is simply a physical orientation owing nothing to any intention. And could it not be said similarly that Darwinian evolution is geared to or aimed at the survival of the fittest? To this extent, then, the notion of aim without intention certainly makes sense.

But in the specific context of the question of the origin of consciousness, is it plausible to suggest that there are natural laws whose existence owes nothing to intention (so does not imply supernatural or pre-existent consciousness) but whose goal or aim or predictable outcome is the appearance of conscious beings?

It will be recalled that the teleological psychophysical theory discussed above may be said to gain some empirical

---

63 *Ibid*, p 93.

support from a certain interpretation of quantum mechanics. The interpretation contemplates that conscious minds in the present somehow contribute to the shape of things in the past and to the manner of their subsequent evolution. This may suggest that the manner in which the laws governing the behaviour of the primal stuff operated in the past may have been shaped by conscious observers at a later time. But *the laws themselves*, with their propensity (realised, as it were, by that later conscious observation) to set in train a process of evolution of conscious observers, *are not regarded as having been constituted or created by a conscious observer or observers*. The potential for the postulated interaction between primal stuff and conscious observers is simply taken to be a characteristic of the way things are, not itself an effect of any conscious intentional action.

Thus even taking account of support derived from quantum mechanics for teleological psychophysical theory, the question remains: is it plausible to suggest that there 'simply are' natural laws whose unintended goal or aim or predictable outcome is the appearance of conscious beings?

The psychophysical answer – plausible or implausible?

It is believed by materialists that there are natural physical laws which, though not yet fully understood, wholly account for the emergence and development of the universe. Starting with a primal physical stuff, more complex and varied physical stuff develops over time. Eventually, chemical reaction produces a molecule capable of reproduction by self-replication, and the process of organic evolution by random mutation and selective advantage is underway. In time, evolution unpredictably and by chance[64] produces conscious beings, but their consciousness and conscious

---

64   See above, note 16.

behaviour is essentially no different from any other behaviour of material phenomena such as non-liquid or non-gaseous molecules becoming liquid or gaseous. Like liquidity and gaseousness, consciousness is merely a feature of the physical.

Here of course (if not much sooner) the psychophysical world view parts company with the materialist. Fundamentally, it is said, consciousness cannot be seen as mere material behaviour. Matter is 'brute', not possessing or connected with reason, intelligence, or sensation.[65] Consciousness is something radically different from brute matter. Moreover, as Nagel argues,[66] cognition cannot be explained in terms of Darwinian selective advantage. 'Mind' as manifested in conscious, intelligent, corporeal beings thus cannot plausibly be regarded as an accidental by-product of a purely material process. If, then, according to psychophysical naturalist theory, consciousness does not emerge by accident, it must emerge in some sense by design:[67] the primal stuff of the universe is not the materialist's purely physical stuff; it is a stuff which has both physical and mental qualities, the natural outcome (end or *telos*) of the latter being the eventual appearance of conscious beings.

This psychophysical naturalist approach tackles what is seen as the implausibility of the 'mind from brute matter' analysis of materialism. But is there a similar implausibility at the heart of psychophysical naturalism? Clearly, teleological laws inherent in and operating upon a mental-physical primal stuff can explain why conscious

---

65 See above, note 6.

66 See above, *Teleology and cognition*.

67 'Design' in the naturalistic sense of a configuration explained by the operation of natural laws – not, of course, in the theistic sense of one divinely intended.

beings in due course appear on earth or wherever else. But is this theory what Nagel refers to as a 'just-so story'[68]? Is it saying no more than that if what we call consciousness is to have a naturalistic explanation, there must be something in the primal stuff and in the laws governing its development which explains it? That 'something' is said itself to be 'mind' or 'consciousness' or 'experience' – familiar words but used in an entirely unfamiliar sense. The mind / consciousness / experience in the primal stuff is in some indefinable way pregnant with (*aimed* or geared, though *not intended,* to produce) the consciousness which is in due course enjoyed by conscious beings. But the consciousness said to be inherent in the primal stuff is not consciousness in the sense enjoyed by conscious beings. Panpsychists, certainly, do not 'hold the view that things like stones and tables are subjects of experience'[69] or that quarks feel and think and plan. But they do hold that everything is composed of primal stuff which is in some sense 'conscious' or 'experiential'. Does this notion of what one might be tempted to call insentient or unconscious consciousness make sense? Certainly, it can seem to make sense if one is indissolubly wedded to a naturalist world view and the choice is between some such theory of primordial consciousness and the 'brute emergence' of the materialist approach.

But at this point, perhaps, re-enter theism.

The plausibility of theism

The theist strongly endorses the psychophysical naturalist's strictures upon materialism but then argues that psychophysical naturalism deserves equally fundamental strictures.

---

68   *Nagel,* p 76.
69   Strawson, *op cit,* p 26.

For the theist too, 'mind' is a basic characteristic of the world, but it is pre-existing, conscious mind. The most plausible explanation of the appearance of conscious beings in the world is, the theist says, that the world itself and the conscious beings who appear in it are the intended creation of a pre-existing, conscious, intelligent being – 'God'. (Of course, many theists accept the evolutionary account of the appearance of conscious beings but would suppose that the primal stuff which God created contained all the propensities, mental and physical, needed to ensure the appearance of such beings.) The psychophysical naturalist will certainly reply that, on this sort of approach, theism is itself a just-so story: you can't explain the appearance of consciousness on earth without postulating pre-existing consciousness – so there must be a pre-existing, conscious, intelligent being or God.

But here a fundamental difference between naturalism and theism may yield a critical distinction. The naturalist universe is finite and physical (even if the physical somehow includes the mental). The theistic universe is, certainly, finite and physical; but God is neither. Theism offers an explanation of mind which views the natural universe as a closed system with an extra-natural origin in the will or intention of a pre-existing, conscious, intelligent being. The cost of embracing this analysis, of course, is accepting as plausible the notion of the extra- (or super-) natural.

Plainly, this is more than a step too far for any self-respecting naturalist. But it is striking that psychophysical naturalism may be seen by materialists as actually providing support for the theistic world view. This is acknowledged with refreshing candour by Richard Lewontin, himself an uncompromising materialist:

It is not that the methods and institutions of science somehow compel us to accept a material explanation of the phenomenal world, but, on the contrary, that we are forced by our *a priori* adherence to material causes to create an apparatus of investigation and a set of concepts that produce material explanations, no matter how counter-intuitive, no matter how mystifying to the uninitiated. Moreover, that materialism is absolute, for we cannot allow a Divine Foot in the door.[70]

The implication is that to entertain as part of one's world view any concepts which – like the mental element in psychophysical naturalism – contemplate *non*-material explanations is to 'allow a Divine Foot in the door'. (And once the door is ajar, other notions might enter which would further undermine the plausibility of materialism – notions including, perhaps, that the mechanism of Darwinian evolution is the product of Divine Mind rather than of a 'Blind Watchmaker'[71].) So, Lewontin is suggesting that if one allows that psychophysical naturalism's fundamental critique of materialism is cogent, one is thereby placing oneself on a slippery slope leading away from naturalism altogether and towards theistic belief. Perhaps, indeed, Nagel's uncertainty about whether the notion of aim without intention makes sense manifests a doubt that naturalism can plausibly accommodate a notion of consciousness to which such aim can be intelligibly ascribed.

---

70 *New York Review of Books*, January 9, 1997 (cited in *Nagel* at p 49, n. 11).

71 Richard Dawkins' book of that name is discussed in 'God and the Design of Organisms', Essay 2 above.

Conclusion

In the end, Nagel's uncertainty about whether the notion of aim without intention makes sense is not enough to prevent him from taking the view in *Mind and Cosmos* that the psychophysical naturalist 'territory between'[72] materialism and theism provides a plausible world view.

But it may be thought that while Nagel's argument against materialism is compelling, his doubts about the coherence of the notion of aim without intention are equally compelling. One may thus be left with the conviction that (as both psychophysical naturalists and theists believe) mind was somehow 'there from the beginning'. One may though, as theists do, find implausible the notion of intentionless, unconscious mind aiming at the emergence of conscious beings. On this basis, with its conception of originating conscious mind, the claims of theism to be a plausible world view are much strengthened.

---

72 *Nagel*, p 22 – cited above, text to note 5.

Postscript

God, Science and Suffering

I. TWO ATHEIST ARGUMENTS

The God/science argument

The three preceding essays attack the atheist-naturalist argument that modern science demonstrates that belief in God is not rational (the 'God/science argument'). The essays seek to show that the discoveries of science are not, in Plantinga's[1] terminology, a 'defeater' for theism and that, far from constituting an insurmountable obstacle to rational belief in God, science may be seen as providing rational support for such belief. Naturalism takes as its basic postulate that the natural world is all that is the case. Once it is understood that this is a postulate – an axiom – which, by definition, cannot be proved, it follows that other world views than naturalism may take a different basic postulate without necessarily being guilty of irrationality. Specifically, it is plainly not irrational (though, as with the naturalist's postulate, it may or may not be correct) to take as the basic postulate of one's world view that the natural world is not all that is the case and that it is a closed system with an extra-natural origin in the will or intention of a pre-existing, conscious, intelligent being, God. Neither cosmology,[2] nor evolutionary theory[3], nor neuroscience[4] provides any ground beyond personal conviction for taking

---

1   Alvin Plantinga, *Where the Conflict Really Lies*, ch 6, *passim*.
2   Essay 1, Consciousness or the Physical Universe – Which Came First?
3   Essay 2, God and the Design of Organisms.
4   Essay 3, Consciousness – Aim Without Intention?

a naturalistic world view: perhaps a *'sensus naturalis'* to oppose the theist's *sensus divinitatis*[5].

The undeserved suffering argument

A quite separate and commonly advanced argument for atheism is that it would in any event be irrational to believe that a world in which there is so much undeserved suffering is the creation of a loving God. This Postscript briefly addresses that argument and its relationship to the God/science argument.

II. HUMAN LIFE AND HUMAN SUFFERING

It is evident that many atheists, in spite of experiencing intense suffering, deserved or undeserved, regard their life as a good. So, Bertrand Russell, who wrote of his 'anguish reaching to the very verge of despair', nevertheless 'found [life] worth living, and would gladly live it again if the chance were offered me'[6]; Ludwig Wittgenstein at the end of a life full of what one biographer refers to as an 'intensity of mental and moral suffering' declared: 'Tell them I've had a wonderful life'[7]; and Stephen Hawking, despite the life-long agony of motor neurone disease, is reported to have said of his life: 'Who could have wished for more?'[8] Such atheists would, presumably, thank God for their life if they believed that he was its source. Certainly they remain fully entitled to decline to believe that their life is a gift of God, but what they cannot rationally do is to insist that their suffering, even though it may be undeserved, of itself precludes rational belief in God. For it would be

---

5   See Preface, above.

6   *Autobiography*, Prologue.

7   Norman Malcolm, *Ludwig Wittgenstein – A Memoir*, p 99.

8   Eckhart Tolle, *A New Earth*, p 213.

irrational to say (as they do) that their life is good in spite of their suffering but then to say that that good life could not rationally be regarded as a gift of God *because of* that suffering.

Of course, atheists may accept all this but say that it is the overwhelming suffering of others less fortunate than themselves which leads them to the conclusion that it would be irrational to believe in a loving God – specifically, in the Judeo-Christian God who is characterised as the loving father of his human children. Against that, it may be pointed out that there are innumerable examples, past and present, of people whose undeserved suffering is of almost unimaginable intensity but who, nevertheless, do believe in a loving God. One may think of Job in the Old Testament, of the innumerable Christian martyrs from biblical times to our own time and of the countless 'ordinary Christians' who retain an undimmed faith despite excruciating fatal illness or other misfortune.

But, still, the question remains of why a loving God would create a world in which so huge a burden of undeserved suffering has to be carried by creatures whom, according to Christian belief, God loves tenderly. Much of that suffering, certainly, results from intentional or uncaring acts of cruelty or unkindness by one human being to another. And it is well understood that much of the perceived goodness of life depends upon the ability of human beings to make moral choices – which may themselves be good or bad. God's decision to grant free will to human beings precludes his intervening even to prevent one person inflicting suffering on another. For if, as Christians believe, God has given humans free will, he has judged that the benefits of free will outweigh the possible or probable consequences of its misuse – in particular in this context its misuse by deliberate and gratuitous infliction of suffering by humans upon other humans.

Yet, some of the very worst of undeserved suffering seems not to flow from the morally bad actions of others: terminal illness in young children, say, or incurable genetic defects leading over years to a horrible and inevitable decline and death. How could a loving God permit or tolerate such sufferings as these? One can perhaps say that God does not 'permit' the suffering which one person intentionally or uncaringly inflicts on another because, by giving people free will, he has disabled himself from intervening. But that surely could not be said of the kind of suffering currently being considered. One might even say that it is possible that God has disabled himself from intervening in this case too because he has made the world as he has made it and in that world such suffering happens. But this invites the riposte that it seems inconceivable that a loving father could create a world of that sort – a world in which it is clearly likely that many of his beloved children will suffer in that way.

A counter-argument here is that a world of the sort which God has created is, precisely, a world in which suffering is a path which must be trodden if beings such as ourselves are to achieve that state of enduring well-being which Buddhists call 'enlightenment' and which Christians call 'blessedness'. It is certainly true that anyone may say with the prophet Isaiah that 'it was for my welfare that I had great bitterness'[9]. But while I can say it for myself, I can never say it for you or anyone else. And, indeed, there are in the world undeserved sufferings so terrible to contemplate that it would seem indecent even to think that they might benefit the sufferer. True, it may be that a world

---

9   Isaiah 38:17.

in which humans find themselves constantly required to suffer in the search for truth, goodness and beauty may have necessarily to be a world in which that suffering can extend – 'collaterally', as it were – to others. For example, the uses to which we have put our acquired knowledge of radioactivity certainly generate some outcomes (e.g. carcinogenic genetic mutations) which lead to much undeserved suffering. But it is precisely this sense that so much undeserved suffering is of this 'collateral' type which leads people to ask how a loving and omniscient creator could countenance it.

Here, then, is the strong basis for the undeserved suffering argument for atheism. And the argument is frequently invoked by contemporary high-profile atheists. For example: 'Asked what he would say if he was confronted by God at the pearly gates of heaven, Stephen Fry replied: "I'd say, bone cancer in children? What's that about? How dare you? How dare you create a world in which there is such misery that is not our fault? It's not right, it's utterly, utterly evil."'[10]

It must be admitted that those who refuse to accept that this kind of undeserved suffering is a defeater for theism, particularly for Christian belief, are hard put to it to raise any cogent argument to support their view.

III. LIFE AFTER DEATH

It is, of course, well understood that in the Christian view of things our death, after a life which is short and characterised by suffering, is not so much an end as the beginning of a new 'life after death'. So far as I can see, this, and this only, provides a basis for justifying Christian belief in the face of the kind of undeserved suffering now being considered.

---

10 *The Independent*, 20 May 2017.

Two questions arise:

(i) *May one rationally believe in life after death?* As noted above, the central argument of the three essays in this book is that science does not establish the irrationality of belief in God. If that is accepted, and one believes in God, surely one may rationally believe in the possibility of life after death: God is a conscious, intelligent, non-material ('spiritual') being who exists outside time and space; may not the conscious, intelligent beings whom God has (in whatever way) created – beings including ourselves – also (in some way) continue to live outside time and space after their earthly demise?

(ii) *If one may rationally believe in life after death, and if one does, how might that belief undermine the undeserved suffering argument as it applies to cases of the sort under discussion?* Consider the account given of life after death in Christianity. Christ, God in human form, 'rises from the dead' three days after he dies, crucified and in physical and mental torment, crying out: 'My God, My God, why have you forsaken me?'[11]. Christ is 'the first of human kind to be born from the dead'[12] but all human beings also will 'rise from death' – the mortal human body in its earthly existence animated by the natural breath of life will be re-born as an immortal body animated by the Spirit of the living God[13]. The short human life characterised by suffering and, in the cases under discussion, largely or wholly untainted by wrong-doing, will pass from this 'veil of tears' into a life without suffering, without end and without limit to its creative development in love of God and of fellow human beings. The Catholic doctrine

---

11   Matthew 27:46; Mk 15:34.
12   Colossians 1:18.
13   1 Corinthians 15:44.

of Purgatory expresses belief in a temporally finite state of human existence between earthly death and heavenly bliss for those many human beings whose capacity for this limitless, creative development in love is, at the time of their death, inhibited by wrong-doing during their earthly lives. This finite period of 'purgative suffering' is seen as removing this inhibition. So, the argument, put with starkest brevity, is that 'the sufferings of this present time are not worth comparing with the glory that is to be revealed to us'[14].

Even on this basis the question remains: why would a loving God permit or tolerate such sufferings as terminal illness in young children or incurable genetic defects leading over years to a horrible and inevitable decline and death? Why, indeed, would a loving God subject all his beloved children to an earthly existence consciously lived in the shadow of impending death? Are such undeserved sufferings regarded by God as a necessary prelude to eternal happiness – and, if so, why? All that we can say (having pointed out above that undeserved suffering may indeed be a necessary feature of the kind of world which a benevolent God might create) is that, if our existence is indeed geared to everlasting heavenly happiness, the rigours of the path are for us all infinitely outweighed by the glory – the splendour and bliss – of the destination.

* * *

While this analysis, if accepted, may undermine the undeserved suffering argument, it is likely, of course, to be at once derided by atheist naturalists as unworthy of consideration by a rational person on the basis that the God/science argument rules out belief in the supernatural

---

14   Romans 8:18.

and the hereafter.[15] But the God/science argument cannot coherently be invoked to reject the life-after-death response to the undeserved suffering argument. This response to that argument may or may not be thought plausible in itself, but logically it cannot be defeated by the God/science argument. For, on the one hand, if the God/science argument is accepted, the undeserved suffering argument is not necessary in order to prove the atheist's case. But, on the other, if the God/science argument is rejected, it is not available as a weapon against the undeserved suffering argument.

IV. ANIMAL SUFFERING[16]

Thus far, the undeserved suffering which has been considered as grounding an argument against the rationality of belief in a loving God has been human suffering. But if, as just suggested, in order to counter this argument in relation to human suffering it is necessary to invoke belief in life after death, would not animal suffering then constitute a formidable and distinct undeserved suffering argument? With reference to animal suffering it has been said that

> it is impossible to call that Being good who, existing prior to the phenomenal universe, and creating it out of the plenitude of infinite power and foreknowledge, endowed it with such properties that its material and

---

15 Though, it may be that many self-proclaimed atheists when approaching death find, with Hamlet, that –

> '... the dread of something after death,
> The undiscovered country, from whose bourn
> No traveller returns, puzzles the will,
> And makes us rather bear those ills we have
> Than fly to others that we know not of ....'

16 Michael J. Murray, *Nature Red in Tooth and Claw*, (Oxford University Press, 2008); hereafter, *Murray*.

moral development must inevitably be attended by the misery of untold millions of sentient creatures for whose existence their creator is ultimately alone responsible.[17]

How can one respond to this? One approach is as follows.

Do animals suffer as humans do?

The key question is whether it is in fact possible to assert that the created universe is 'endowed ... with such properties that its ... development must inevitably be attended by the misery of untold millions of sentient creatures'. The view that it is seems to take for granted that at least some species of higher animals suffer misery as humans do. But in fact we do not know this. We do not know that a gazelle captured and being eaten by a pursuing cheetah suffers as a human being suffers who has, say, been caught and is being eaten by a polar bear. The gazelle – and other higher animals in similar situations – may or may not suffer in that way. Before seeing why they may not, it must be said that most humans believe intuitively that they do. I am not suggesting that anyone should modify their behaviour towards such animals and abandon a humane attitude towards them. The issue is whether we know enough about animal suffering to count that suffering as a defeater for theistic belief. If it turns out that we do not, so that the animal suffering argument is not a defeater, there would still be no basis for discarding our notion that it is inhumane and immoral for us to treat animals with what we consider (on the basis of our intuitive beliefs) to be cruelty.

What basis, then, have we to doubt that (at least) some higher animals suffer *as humans do*?[18] Many animal

---

17 The American philosopher John Fiske's, *Miscellaneous Writings*, 1904, cited in *Murray* at p 4.

18 *Murray*, ch 2.

species have brains and central nervous systems which are physiologically so similar to those of humans that it seems difficult to doubt that those animal species can and do experience pain like ours. But neuro-physiology shows that, in many species, distinct neural pathways have different functions in translating potentially harmful physical stimuli into the experience of pain: one pathway which detects a noxious stimulus (as a vehicle's rear sensors detect the proximity of a hazard) and a second (generated in the prefrontal cortex region of the brain) which attaches the 'affective' response of felt pain. Prefrontal cortex development differs from species to species and it may be the case that different levels of development in different mammalian brains may deliver different levels of 'felt' pain. This said, the neuro-physiological similarity between the brains of humans and, in particular, those of humanoid primates suggests a very close susceptibility to felt pain.

But more broadly on the question of whether – and which – animals may be said to suffer as humans do, one must revert to the fundamental question explored in Essay 3 above: can consciousness be exhaustively described and understood in purely physical terms? The materialist[19] atheist says yes, and thus regards as incoherent Nagel's thesis[20] that no species of animal can experience 'what it is like to be' another. The materialist finds this incoherent because, for him, experience – consciousness – is nothing more than a feature of certain brain states just as liquidity is simply a feature of the arrangement of atoms of hydrogen and oxygen which we call water.[21] For the materialist, talk of different levels of consciousness eventuating from

19 On materialism, see Essay 3, above, p 64.
20 See Essay 3, note 24, above.
21 *Ibid,* text to note 4.

essentially similar physical phenomena (e.g. certain mammalian brains) is nonsense. But if consciousness is a phenomenon in itself, explicable ultimately in non-physical terms, the question of the extent to which humans can know what it is like to be, say, a gazelle remains open and important. Humans certainly enjoy greater cognitive powers than any other species – powers which deliver a perhaps unique self-consciousness, essential for awareness of the undesirability of experiencing pain stimuli.[22] Our experience tells us that those powers also deliver to us enhanced levels of both pleasure and pain: so, for example, our joy in many circumstances is intensified by our powers of both recollection and anticipation – indeed, as suggested above, sometimes intensified in part by awareness of past suffering overcome; and our pain in many other circumstances is likewise intensified. In such circumstances we may suppose that our suffering is greater than that of gazelles or of cats and dogs. Thus, critically, on the question of whether animal suffering is a defeater for theism, one remains entitled to be at least agnostic on the question of whether all or any animals suffer as humans do. Only an unequivocally affirmative answer to that question will carry the weight required to be carried by the argument that animal suffering rules out rational belief in divine benevolence – that is if the foundational premise of the argument is precisely that animals do suffer 'as we do'.

Animal pain and divine benevolence

But perhaps 'equivalence of suffering' is not the foundational premise of the argument. Perhaps the argument that animal suffering rules out rational belief in divine benevolence

---

22   See *Murray,* pp 55-57.

can stand simply on the basis that animal suffering *of any sort* cannot be justified by the arguments advanced above to justify human suffering – especially the life after death argument which was presented as the decisive argument there.

It is true that there is a long and strong tradition in Protestant Christian thought[23] which does indeed invoke the life after death argument in the case of animal suffering. Luther, Calvin and Wesley all seem to have believed that, as one of the foremost contemporary philosophers of the Christian religion, Keith Ward, has said:[24]

> Theism would be falsified if physical death was the end, for then there could be no justification for the existence of this world. However, if one supposes that every sentient being has an endless existence, which offers the prospect of supreme happiness, it is surely true that the sorrows and troubles of this life will seem very small by comparison. Immortality, for animals as well as humans, is a necessary condition of any acceptable theodicy[25]....

It was suggested above that the level of a sentient being's capacity to suffer – and, in some way, to profit from suffering – is related to its level of cognitive capacity. May it not also be indicative of the level of that 'happiness suited to its state'[26] which it will enjoy hereafter? Certainly, the notion of *post mortem* survival of animals, like that of

---

23 *Murray,* pp 123-4.

24 See *Murray,* p 122.

25 I.e., a justification of theistic belief in the face of the existence of suffering. This notion of animal immortality has obvious affinities with Buddhist teaching on the nature and value of all sentient beings.

26 'The General Deliverance', a sermon of Samuel Wesley cited in *Murray* at p 123.

human beings, reflects the core Judeo-Christian perception that 'God is not God of the dead, but of the living'[27].

* * *

The fact remains that, immortality for animals or not, we simply do not know enough about human, let alone animal, consciousness to be clear about what, in the case of animal suffering, we are seeking to justify in order to counter the atheist's undeserved suffering argument. That argument is not a defeater for theism in the case of human suffering. The issue of animal suffering remains cloudy and, in our present state of knowledge, is likewise insufficient to count as an insurmountable obstacle to rational belief in God.

---

27   Matthew 22:32; Mark 12:27; Luke 20:38.

Index